Cast from the
MOUNTAIN OF GLORY
to the *LAKE OF FIRE*

THE HARLOT DRAGON

ALAN T. HARRIS

ISBN Softback: 979-8-9922525-0-7
ISBN eBook: 979-8-9922525-1-4
Library of Congress Control Number: 9798992252507

All Scripture is taken from the Authorized King James Version of the Holy Bible. The bolding and underlining of certain words are added by the author for emphasis and do not represent an alteration of the public domain text.

THE HARLOT DRAGON will dive deeper into the beginnings of creation to reveal this hidden story within the scriptures of the King James Bible. *"It is the glory of God to conceal a thing: but the honour of kings is to search out a matter." Proverbs 25:2*

What You Will Learn

Who was Lucifer, why did he fall, and what was his goal?
- Why was the Earth renewed?
- Where do angels reside?
- Who is Rahab?
- Who is Leviathan?
- Who are the devils and unclean spirits (demons)?
- Who is the Lord of Host?
- How will this war end?

1. Bible 2. Salvation 3. Judgment 4. Creation 5. Lucifer 6. Dragon
7. Leviathan 8. Harlot
I Harris, Alan T. II THE HARLOT DRAGON

THE HARLOT DRAGON may be purchased at special quantity discounts for churches, colleges, universities, educational, or resale purposes. We also offer reprints of specific chapters or the entire book and Rights or Licensing Agreements. For more information, contact Alan at lionstarpub@gmail.com

Interior Layout: Megan Leid
Publishing Advisor: Mel Cohen www.inspiredauthorspress.com
Publisher: LionStar Publishing LLC
Website: https://lookingforthatblessedhope.com/
Printed in the United States of America

CONTENTS

DEDICATION

To my wife Sandra, my son Isaac,
and my daughter Leah

ACKNOWLEDGEMENT

It is with the help and direction of the Lord Jesus and by His grace that I was able to compose this book. To the King of Kings, I give thanks for His Word and allowing circumstances in my life to change favorably for the time and environment needed to write.

With the love, support, and encouragement of my beloved wife Sandra, I endeavored to finish the mission. Thanks to my son Isaac, for reading each chapter as I wrote it, and to my daughter Leah, for helping with the graphics.

Thanks to Michael Pearl for his many wonderful books I have read, influencing and encouraging me to write my own.

It is my hope that many will come to know and believe on the name of Jesus through this book.

PREFACE

The unsaved man stands before the cross, convicted of his sin, knowing he needs a Savior to cover his sin. He is fed milk to learn the principles of the doctrine of Christ, the shed blood of Christ, salvation, faith, baptism, the resurrection, etc. From there, it is the responsibility of the saved man to move to the other side of the cross, looking forward to the deeper things of God and partaking in strong meat. We are commanded to do so as the writer of Hebrews states: *"Therefore **leaving the principles** of the doctrine of Christ, **let us go on unto perfection; not laying again** the foundation of repentance from dead works, and of faith toward God, Of the doctrine of baptisms, and of laying on of hands, and of resurrection of the dead, and of eternal judgment. And this will we do, if God permit"* *Hebrews 6:1-3.* Once saved, how many Christians take the time to do this? Hebrews also makes this clear when speaking about the order of Melchisedec.

> *"And being made perfect, he became the author of eternal salvation unto all them that obey*

him; Called of God an high priest after the order of Melchisedec. Of whom we have many things to say, and hard to be uttered, seeing ye are dull of hearing. For when for the time ye ought to be teachers, ye have need that one teach you again which be the first principles of the oracles of God; and are become such as have need of milk, and not of strong meat. For every one that useth milk is unskilful in the word of righteousness: for he is a babe. But strong meat belongeth to them that are of full age, even those who by reason of use have their senses exercised to discern both good and evil." Hebrews 5:9-14

Herein is the ongoing historical issue, especially in the world today: most people, including the unsaved and many Christians, cannot discern between good and evil due to a lack of a deep understanding of the scriptures. Paul states in one of the most important and powerful verses in the Bible, *"For we wrestle **not against flesh and blood, but against** principalities, against powers, against the rulers of the darkness of this world, against spiritual wickedness in high places" Ephesians 6:12.* A cursory reading of the Word will not suffice to understand this ideology.

The Bible commands us to "rightly divide" the Word, study the scriptures daily, and pray that our eyes would be opened. *"These were nobler than those in Thessalonica, in that they received the word with **all readiness of mind,** and **searched the scriptures daily,** whether those things were so"* Acts 17:11. *"**Study to shew thyself approved** unto God, a workman that needeth not to be ashamed, **rightly dividing** the word of truth"* 2 Timothy 2:15. *"Open thou mine eyes, that I may **behold wondrous things** out of thy law"* Psalm 119:18.

God conceals hidden truths within his Word, and it is our responsibility to discover them. *"It is the glory of God to **conceal a thing: but the honour of kings is to search out a matter"** Proverbs 25:2.* However, this cannot be done efficiently unless one uses the King James Version (KJV). Corruption of God's Word began in Genesis 3:1, resulting in multiple versions and translations of the Bible, each projecting a different message from the KJV. It is one of the strongest tactics of Satan: promote deception and keep the truth of God's Word from the masses.

*"Now the serpent was more subtil than any beast of the field which the LORD God had made. And he said unto the woman, **Yea, hath God said,** Ye shall not eat of every tree of the garden?"*
Genesis 3:1

*"When any one heareth the **word of the kingdom, and understandeth it not,** then cometh the wicked one, and catcheth away that which was*

sown in his heart. This is he which received seed
by the way side."
Matthew 13:19

The Word of God defines itself from within the text, and the KJV is God's perfect, pure Word. *"The **words of the LORD are pure words**: as silver tried in a furnace of earth, **purified seven times**" Psalms 12:6. "**Every word of God is pure**: he is a shield unto them that put their trust in him. **Add thou not unto his words, lest he reprove thee, and thou be found a liar**" Proverbs 30:5-6.* How can the previous verses be accurate with multiple versions of the Bible?

In late 2023, a discovery was made by a brother in Australia. He found if you added all the words in the KJV bible, including the words of the verses, the chapter, verse numbers, full titles of each book, Psalm superscriptions, the Epistle colophons, and the cover text, one would arrive at the number 823,543 or 7 to the 7th power. 7x7x7x7x7x7x7. The first and last verses of the Bible, Genesis 1:1 & Revelation 22:21, have the exact number of letters, vowels, and consonants. Jesus speaks of a jot or tittle, meaning even the smallest of matters matter. *"For verily I say unto you, Till heaven and earth pass, **one jot or one tittle shall** in no wise pass from the law, till all be fulfilled." Matthew 5:18. "Now to Abraham and his seed were the promises made. He saith not, And to* *seeds, as of many; but as of one, And to thy seed, which is Christ." Galatians 3:16.* These two verses of Matthew and Galatians also have the same number of letters, vowels, and consonants. In Galatians, the Lord points out that a single letter "s" in the word "seeds" is relevant and matters to the correct interpretation of scripture.

God is not limited to the Hebrew of the Old Testament and Greek of the New Testament to articulate his Word. No language is too rich or vague for the Holy Ghost. The common hypothesis of using a vernacular language to preserve scripture cannot be done, but only the original languages can be used for accuracy is incorrect. There are problems within the original languages. For example, vernacular translations were used to preserve some scriptures of the Old Testament. *"...they pierced my hands and my feet" Psalm 22:16* KJV versus most Hebrew manuscripts that read, *"...like a lion, they are at my hands and my feet" MT V17.* Turning to the ancient manuscripts to correct the Bible into multiple translations when we already have it in the perfect KJV also assumes God did not preserve his Word.

> *"Heaven and earth shall pass away: but my words shall not pass away."*
> *Luke 21:33.*

> *"And they were all amazed and marvelled, saying one to another, Behold, are not all these which*

*speak Galilæans? And how hear we every man in
our own tongue, wherein we were born?"*
Acts 2:7-8

Numerous perfect numeric patterns within the KJV cannot
be found in any other version. Brother Brandon from the
U.S. has created multiple videos showing the perfection of
the KJV. You can find him on YouTube @TruthisChrist.
If you watch just one video, choose *"The 666th Mention
of Jesus is a False Prophet"*. Brandon has also created a
very powerful search database that this author has used
extensively to write this book: KJVcode.com. The words
of Daniel ring clearly in these last days. *"But thou, O
Daniel, shut up the words, and seal the book, even **to the
time of the end**: many shall run to and fro, and **knowledge
shall be increased"*** Daniel 12:4.

INTRODUCTION

War for the Kingdom. That is the underlying theme of the Bible. An ancient galactic battle that started with the fall of Lucifer, which introduced sin and death into God's creation. The war will end with the 2nd battle of Gog and Magog and the defeat of the final enemy, death. *"The last enemy that shall be destroyed is death"* 1 Corinthians 15:26.

> *"And when the thousand years are expired, Satan shall be loosed out of his prison, And shall go out to deceive the nations which are in the four quarters of the earth, Gog and Magog, to gather them together to battle: the number of whom is as the sand of the sea. And they went up on the breadth of the earth, and compassed the camp of the saints about, and the beloved city: and fire came down from God out of heaven, and devoured them. And the devil that deceived them was cast into the lake of fire and brimstone, where the beast*

and the false prophet are, and shall be tormented
day and night for ever and ever."
Revelation 20:7-10

It is a love story of a King who wishes to share his perfect, unconditional love with a family for eternity. Like any real love story, the knight's mission to rescue his princess from the enemy's hand, is one daunted with turmoil and destruction. It includes the history of Lucifer, a servant created and crowned for the highest position of the kingdom under the King and given dominion over the earth. Lucifer rebelled against his King and took an untold number of the King's subjects with him. After his rebellion, the King of Heaven and Earth created another race of beings called man, and gave him dominion over the earthly kingdom. However, man sinned and lost his dominion, and Satan once again held dominion over the earth. But God intends for man to rule the coming world, and dominion will change hands once again, as the angels testify below.

*"For unto the angels **hath he not put in subjec-***
***tion** the world to come, whereof we speak. But*
one in a certain place testified, saying, What is
man, that thou art mindful of him? or the son of
man, that thou visitest him? Thou madest him a
*little lower than the angels; thou **crownedst him***
with glory and honour, and didst set him over the

*works of thy hands: Thou hast put **all things in
subjection under his feet**. For in that he put all in
subjection under him, **he left nothing** that is not
put under him. But now we see **not yet** all things
put under him."*
Hebrews 2:5-8

The King, in his mercy, allowed the new creation of man
to choose—by their own free will—either to live in his
Kingdom for eternity through his only begotten son Jesus,
or to forsake the Son and rebel in wickedness, forever separated from the King. *"For God is my King of old, **working
salvation in the midst of the earth**" Psalms 74:12.*

*"But we see **Jesus**, who was made a little lower
than the angels for the suffering of death,
crowned with glory and honour; that he by the
grace of God should **taste death for every man**.
For it became him, for whom are all things, and
by whom are all things, in **bringing many sons
unto glory**, to make the **captain of their salvation**
perfect through sufferings."*
Hebrews 2:9-10

The Creator King, in his omnipotence, knows the end
from the beginning.

*"**Declaring the end from the beginning**, and from
ancient times the things that are not yet done,*

> *saying, My counsel shall stand, and I will do all*
> *my pleasure:"*
> Isaiah 46:10

The Bible, written for mankind, is a roadmap to all of life, navigating the ongoing battles and how to access the eternal coming Kingdom. It chronicles the beginning stages of man and ends with the defeat of all enemies of the Kingdom. Along the way are the constant battles between good and evil. Battles between what the Apostle Paul describes here: *"For we wrestle not against flesh and blood, but against* **principalities,** *against* **powers,** *against the* **rulers of the darkness** *of this world, against* **spiritual wickedness in** *high places" Ephesians 6:12.* Understanding this verse is vital to understanding the underlining theme of the Bible. It is Satan and his fallen that battle with the holy angels, the ministers of God, throughout man's history to thwart the plan of God and His coming Kingdom of Heaven on Earth.

> *The LORD hath prepared his throne in the heav-*
> *ens; and his kingdom ruleth over all. Bless the*
> *LORD, ye his angels, that excel in strength,* **that**
> **do his commandments, hearkening unto the voice**
> **of his word.** *Bless ye the LORD, all ye his hosts;*
> **ye ministers of his,** *that do his pleasure Psalms*
> *103:19-21*

These heavenly beings, which the Apostle Paul speaks of, have a history prior to the creation of man, the generations of old. Man was not given their complete history in a book; however, a student of the Word can find nuggets and tidbits along the way to piece together much of this history as this book attempts to do. The galactic battle that shattered the solar system and left the earth in ruins resulted in a renewal of Earth and the beginning of "time"; a 7,000-year countdown of man's history on Earth ending in eternity once again.

CHAPTER 1

SEVEN DAYS

*"In the beginning God created the heaven and the earth. And the earth was without form, and void; and **darkness was upon the face of the deep. And the Spirit of God moved** upon the face of the waters."* Genesis 1:1-2

The seven-day creation is the renewing of the face of the earth after the destruction that ensued in Genesis 1:2. *"Thou **sendest forth thy spirit**, they are **created**: and **thou renewest** the face of the earth"* Psalm 104:30. God is light with no darkness in him; how could he begin the creation in the darkness from Genesis 1:2 unless something caused the removal of light? *"This then is the message which we have heard of him, and declare unto you, that **God is light, and in him is no darkness at all**"* 1 John 1:5. Where did the darkness come from? Darkness comes from the removal of light. This renewing of the "dead" earth is a picture of the coming resurrection; the earth submerged under the deep as one dead to be risen with a renewal of the body.

Genesis 1:1-2 occurred before the events of day 1. The seven-day account does not mention angels, cherubs, and other heavenly beings. They had already been created. The angels, or "morning stars," were present when God "created" the earth "in the beginning." God asked Job, *"Where wast thou **when I laid the foundations** of the earth? declare, if thou hast understanding. Who hath laid the measures thereof, if thou knowest? or who hath stretched the line upon it? Whereupon are the foundations thereof fastened? or who laid the corner stone thereof; **When the morning stars sang** together, and all the **sons of God shouted for joy?"** Job 38:4-7.*

The key to understanding the creation account of Genesis starting in verse 3 of chapter 1, is to discern the difference between the words *"**created**"* and *"**made**."* Only God can create; to create means to bring forth something out of nothing. When something is "made," it is formed from existing material. Man can "make" things from material that God created. The KJV clearly distinguishes between the two words, as noted. One can also note the word "made" was used three times to a single entry of "created" in the first paragraph of Genesis 2, perhaps suggesting three-quarters or more of this renewal act was "made" rather than created.

*"Thus the heavens and the earth were finished, and all the host of them. And on the seventh day God ended his work which he had **made**; and he rested on the seventh day from all his work which he had **made**. And God blessed the seventh day, and sanctified it: because that in it he had rested from all his work which God **created** and **made**."*
Genesis 2:1-3

Day 1 – "And God said let there be light." On the first day, God returned the light previously removed in Genesis 1:2. Why? Because all the light of the earth was extinguished, and the earth was submerged under the darkness of the deep. God had commanded the sun not to rise. Before Lucifer's fall, light from the stars of heaven (they were much closer to earth) and possibly Lucifer himself lit the earth by reflecting God's glory via the precious stones embedded within him. God removed the light of His glory, and the light was quenched once it became contaminated with sin, engulfing heaven and earth with total darkness. *"Which **commandeth** the **sun**, and it **riseth not**; and **sealeth up** the **stars**." Job 9:7 "And from the **wicked their light is withholden**, and the **high arm shall be broken**" Job 38:15.* In the new Heaven and Earth, God himself will be the light. *"And the city had **no need of the sun, neither of the moon**, to shine in it: for the **glory of God did lighten it**, and the **Lamb is the light thereof**"*

Revelation 21:23. Using the light from his own glory until day four, God then separated the light from the darkness. *"Who **coverest thyself with light** as with a garment: who **stretchest out the heavens** like a **curtain**:" Psalm 104:2* (the heavens were stretched on day two). As a result of sin, darkness was to remain in the creation until all enemies had been destroyed.

God did not say the darkness was "good," rather only the light. The night represents sleep and death; the day, waking and rising, is a daily reminder of the coming resurrection. God calling for light from the darkness on day one is the first instance of a picture representing salvation to be used throughout the Bible. *"For God, **who commanded the light to shine out of darkness**, hath shined in our hearts, to give the **light of the knowledge of the glory** of God in the face of **Jesus Christ**" 2 Corinthians 4:6.* Keep in mind God instituted this on day one before the creation of Adam and the first sin of man. A study of the word "darkness" in the KJV will reveal nothing positive. The entire earth at Genesis 1:2, "void and without form," was a planet of death; it was when Hell was formed beneath and would remain. *"Are not my days few? cease then, and let me alone, that I may take comfort a little, Before I go whence I shall not return, even to the **land of darkness** and the **shadow of death**; A **land of darkness, as darkness itself**; and of the shadow of death, **without any order**, and where the **light is as darkness**" Job 10:20-22.* Paul says,

*"Ye are all the children of light, and the children of the day: **we are not of the night, nor of darkness**" 1 Th. 5:5.*

> *"And God said, Let there be light: and there was light. And God saw the **light, that it was good:** and God **divided** the light from the darkness. And God called the light Day, and the darkness he called Night. And the evening and the morning were the first day." Genesis 1:3-5*

Day 2 – The biblical number two represents divisions as in the division between good and evil. Before day two, there was only one Heaven. Yes, a single letter matters in the KJV, as seen in Galatians 3:16. *"In the beginning God created the **heaven** and the earth" Genesis 1:1.* The firmament, or the second heaven, was made on day two and stretched out, creating the universe. *"I have **made** the earth, and **created** man upon it: I, even my hands, have **stretched out the heavens**, and all their host have I commanded." Isaiah 45:12. "Which commandeth the sun, and it riseth not; and sealeth up the stars. Which alone **spreadeth out the heavens**, and **treadeth** upon the **waves of the sea.**" Job 9:7-8.* The morning stars, the angels, previously shined in an unstretched heaven that held clouds and flying birds. We know this from Lucifer's mention of "clouds" in his fatal statement, *"For thou hast said in thine heart, I will ascend into heaven, I will **exalt my throne above the stars** *of God*: *I will sit also upon the mount of the congregation, in the sides of the north: I will ascend* **above the heights of the clouds**;" *Isaiah 14:13-14.* On day two, God moved His chambers into the third heaven (Psalm 104:3 below).

Genesis **verse 2** informs of the great destruction that ensued because of a **division** between good and evil. *"**And the earth was without form, and void; and darkness was upon the face of the deep***. *And the Spirit of God moved upon the face of the waters.* " No land is yet visible until the third day, buried under the deep.

> *"For this they willingly are ignorant of, that by the word of God the heavens were of old, and* **the earth standing out of the water and in the water***: Whereby* **the world that then was***, being overflowed with water,* **perished.** "
> 2 Peter 3:5-6

> *"Hath in these last days spoken unto us by his Son, whom he hath appointed heir of all things, by whom also he made the* **worlds.** "
> Hebrews 1:2 *(worlds, plural).*

Many attribute the verse in 2 Peter above to Noah's flood; however, all the earth did not perish. Noah and his family were spared. On day two, God separated these waters of death by placing the waters above and below the universe. God called the firmament heaven (universe).

This constitutes the three heavens we know today. The sky is where the clouds reside, and birds fly, the heaven of the universe, and Heaven, the present home of God, which is the only day of the seven that *was not* called "good" by God. Notice these waters were already present before day one, and there is no mention of their creation as they had already been created in Genesis 1:1.

> *"And God said, Let there be a **firmament in the midst** of the waters, and let it **divide** the waters from the waters. And God **made the firmament**, and divided the waters which were under the firmament from the waters which were above the firmament: and it was so. And God called the firmament Heaven. And the evening and the morning were the second day."*
> *Genesis 1:6-8*

The waters placed above the firmament would be used again during the flood of Noah to account for the massive volume of water rained down upon the earth for forty days. *"For yet seven days, and I will **cause it to rain upon the earth forty days and forty nights**; and every living substance that I have made will I destroy from off the face of the earth" Genesis 7:4. "The fountains also of the deep and **the windows of heaven were stopped**, and the rain from heaven was restrained;" Genesis 8:2.* It is a literal sea, frozen like crystal or glass under the throne of God. The Lord's chariot, as described in Ezekiel, presents a vision of the crystal above the Cherubim. In Revelation, John is taken before the throne of God, which was upon a sea of glass.

> "Who **layeth the beams of his chambers in the waters**: who maketh the clouds his chariot: who walketh upon the wings of the wind:"
> Psalm 104:3

> "Praise him, ye heavens of heavens, and **ye waters that be above the heavens.**"
> Psalms 148:4

> "And the likeness of the **firmament** upon the heads of the living creature was as the colour of the terrible **crystal**, stretched forth over their heads above."
> Ezekiel 1:22

> "And above the **firmament** that was over their heads was the likeness of a **throne**, as the appearance of a sapphire stone: and upon the likeness of the throne was the likeness as the appearance of a man above upon it."
> Ezekiel 1:26

> "And before the throne, there was a **sea of glass**

*like unto **crystal**: and in the midst of the throne, and round about the throne, were four beasts full of eyes before and behind."*
Revelation 4:6

*"And I saw as it were a **sea of glass** mingled with fire: and them that had gotten the victory over the beast, and over his image, and over his mark, and over the number of his name, **stand on the sea of glass**, having the harps of God."*
Revelation 15:2

The waters above the firmament could also be used to keep the fallen ones from entering the presence of God unless **called** into His presence. The disembodied spirit of Satan and the fallen ones still have access to Heaven, but only when God calls for an assembly of the host. When a war breaks out in Heaven, possibly at one of these assemblies, they are finally cast out permanently by Michael and his angels (Revelation 12:7-8). Created beings with a spirit do not have the power to separate their spirit from the body at will. Satan, as a disembodied spirit, used a serpent in the Garden of Eden to speak with Eve just as he entered as a spirit into the body of Judas to betray Jesus. *"And after the sop **Satan entered** into him. Then said Jesus unto him, That thou doest, do quickly" John 13:27.* When a being is called, they come to **present** themselves before the one that calls. This scenario can be seen in the book of Job and 1 Kings.

> *"Again there was a day when the sons of God* **came to present** *themselves before the Lord, and Satan* **came also** *among them* **to present himself** *before the Lord."*
> *Job 2:2*

> *"And he said, Hear thou therefore the word of the LORD: I saw the LORD sitting on his throne, and* **all the host of heaven standing by him** *on his right hand and on his left. And the LORD said, Who shall persuade Ahab, that he may go up and fall at Ramoth–gilead? And one said on this manner, and another said on that manner. And there came forth* **a spirit,** *and stood before the LORD, and said, I will persuade him. And the LORD said unto him, Wherewith? And he said, I will go forth, and I will be* **a lying spirit** *in the mouth of all his prophets. And he said, Thou shalt persuade him, and prevail also: go forth, and do so. Now therefore, behold, the LORD hath put a lying spirit in the mouth of all these thy prophets, and the LORD hath* **spoken evil** *concerning thee."*
> *1 Kings 22:19-23*

In 1 Kings, the host of heaven is standing by the Lord. A spirit, or one that is disembodied, comes forth and suggests becoming a lying spirit in the mouth of the prophets. The Lord creates evil when it is warranted, and he uses the lying spirit to speak evil against King Ahab. *"I form the light, and create darkness: I make peace, and create evil: I the LORD do all these things." Isaiah 45:7*

In Revelation, after the Lord defeated all enemies and sent them to the lake of fire, John witnessed a new heaven and new earth, and there was no more sea. The singular form of "heaven" is used again, as in Genesis 1:1. The sea mentioned here may well be the waters currently above the firmament, no longer needed as the enemy has been vanquished. The seas here on earth are perhaps one of the Lord's most majestic creations.

> *"And I saw a new heaven and a new earth: for the first heaven and the first earth were passed away; and there was no more sea."*
> *Revelation 21:1*

Day 3 – God commanded the dry land to appear as he gathered the waters under the firmament into the seas. *"To him that stretched out the earth above the waters: for his mercy endureth for ever" Psalms 136:6*. The previously created dry land of the earth was hidden under the depths of the deep in Genesis 1:2.

*"**And God said, Let** the waters **under the heaven** be gathered together unto one place, and let the **dry land appear**: and it was so. And God called the dry land Earth; and the gathering together of the waters called he Seas: and God saw that it was good."*
Genesis 1:9-10.

*"And God said, Let the earth bring forth grass, the herb yielding seed, and the fruit tree yielding fruit **after his kind, whose seed is in itself, upon the earth**: and it was so. And the earth brought forth grass, and herb yielding seed **after his kind**, and the tree yielding fruit, whose seed **was in itself**, after his kind: and God saw that it was good."*
Genesis 1:11-12

On day three, God brought forth the grasses, herbs, and trees. Three times, God mentions "after his kind." Why is that? Because much of the vegetation had been genetically corrupted by the fallen, he only allowed that which was perfect to emerge. "Whose seed is in itself, upon the earth." Did you catch that? The seed of plants lies within the plant itself and these plants were already lying "upon the earth" covered under the water. God called them forth.

Day 4 – On this day, God "made" the sun, moon, and stars and set them in their proper place. As we saw on day two, God moved his chambers to the highest Heaven (see Psalm 104:3) but will once again live among his creation at the coming of the new Jerusalem. *"And I John saw the holy city, **new Jerusalem**, coming down from God out of heaven, prepared as a bride adorned for her **husband**" Revelation 21:2.* Day four instituted the beginning of time as we know it. Time did not exist in the previous world. However, God, in his foreknowledge, knew Adam would eventually sin and started the 7,000-year countdown to the ultimate judgment day. The universe is covered in blackness and devoid of life, a testimony to Lucifer's sin that affected the whole of creation. *"For we know that **the whole creation** groaneth and travaileth in pain together until now" Romans 8:22.*

> *"And God said, Let there be lights in the firmament of the heaven to divide the day from the night; and let them be for signs, and for seasons, and **for days, and years**: And let them be for lights in the firmament of the heaven to give light upon the earth: and it was so. And God **made two great lights**; the greater light to rule the day, and the lesser light to rule the night: he **made the stars** also. And God **set them in the firmament** of the heaven to give light upon the earth, And to rule over the day and over the night, and to divide the light from the darkness: and God saw that it was*

good. And the evening and the morning were the fourth day."
Genesis 1:14-19

Day 5 – Every word of the KJV is essential. On this day, the Lord uses the words "hath life" when he commands the waters to fill abundantly with moving creatures. The opposite of life is death. *"**Dead things** are **formed** from under the waters, and the **inhabitants** thereof." Job 26:5.* Notice the word "formed" versus "created" in the prior verse. The floods of Noah and the pre-Adamic world did not destroy the mutated creatures formed by the fallen ones when they genetically corrupted what God had created in his goodness on the earth during those times. Have you ever seen pictures of the otherworldly creatures at the lowest depths of the sea? They look not of this world. There is further evidence of this corruption in the book of Revelation. *"And the second angel poured out his vial upon the sea; and it became as the blood of a dead man: and **every living soul died** in the sea. And the third angel poured out his vial upon **the rivers and fountains of waters**; and they became blood. And I heard the **angel of the waters** say, Thou art righteous, O Lord, which art, and wast, and shalt be, because thou hast judged thus" Revelation 16:3-5.* All life in the sea will be eliminated towards the end of the Tribulation to destroy these ancient creatures of abomination. Then, at the Great

White Throne judgment, the dead of the sea are given up, as are those in Hell. There is a clear distinction between these two locations for the dead. *"And the **sea gave up the dead** which were in it; and **death and hell delivered up the dead** which were in them: and they were judged every man according to their works" Revelation 20:13.* The dead of the sea are alive but without life. Only that which has the "Spirit of life" has life; only God can create and give it. *"And after three days and an half the **Spirit of life** from God entered into them, and they stood upon their feet; and great fear fell upon them which saw them" Revelation 11:11. "The Spirit of God hath made me, and the breath of the Almighty hath given me **life**" Job 33:4. "By the word of the LORD were the heavens made; and **all the host** of them by the **breath** of his mouth" Psalm 33:6.*

> *"And God said, Let the waters bring forth abundantly the moving creature that **hath life**, and fowl that may fly above the earth in the open firmament of heaven. And God **created great whales, and every living creature that moveth**, which the waters brought forth abundantly, after their kind, and every winged fowl after his kind: and God saw that it was good. And God blessed them, saying, Be fruitful, and multiply, and fill the waters in the seas, and let fowl multiply in the earth. And the evening and the morning were the fifth day." Genesis 1:20-23.*

Day 6 – Again, the Lord uses the word "living" to describe the creatures of the earth. *"And God said, Let the earth bring forth the **living creature** after his kind, cattle, and creeping thing, and beast of the earth after his kind: and it was so"* Genesis 1:24. During the time of Noah and the pre-Adamic earth, the land animals were also corrupted. Satan's reptilian kingdom of dinosaurs during the pre-Adamic world and the abhorred giants and other creatures of Noah's day made during the Genesis 6 account. All these "dead" genetically corrupted land creatures, including the ones God had created, were destroyed in the two floods.

Man is also created and made on the sixth day. He is made/formed from the dust of the earth and created with a soul and spirit. *"And the LORD God **formed** man of the dust of the ground, and breathed into his nostrils the **breath of life**; and man became a living **soul**"* Genesis 2:7. The Lord speaks with his council of angels and determines to make man in "our image." Unlike the cherubim and seraphim, angels were created in the image of God. The plurality of the conversation in the scripture below is not the Trinity discussing amongst themselves. For the Trinity are three, yet one and in perfect harmony; never a need to confer within themselves on a matter. There is only one authority in Heaven. The angels were present when God "created" the earth (Job 38:7) and are present once again with the renewal of the earth after witnessing the cosmic battle between good and evil.

*"And God said, Let us **make man** in **our** image, after **our** likeness: and let them have dominion over the fish of the sea, and over the fowl of the air, and over the cattle, and over all the earth, and over every creeping thing that creepeth upon the earth. So God **created man** in his own image, in the image of God created he him; male and female created he them. And God blessed them, and God said unto them, Be fruitful, and multiply, and **replenish the earth, and subdue it**: and **have dominion** over the fish of the sea, and over the fowl of the air, and over every living thing that moveth upon the earth."*
Genesis 1:26-28

Herein is one of the most overlooked words in the bible. God told Adam and Eve to "replenish the earth." Meaning, to re-populate the earth as it previously was and to subdue it, taking authority of the living creatures on the planet, a responsibility once given to Lucifer. *"And the LORD God **planted a garden eastward in Eden**; and there he put the man whom he had formed. And out of the ground made the LORD God to grow every tree that is pleasant to the sight, and good for food; the tree of life also **in the midst** of the garden, and the tree of knowledge of **good and evil**"* *Genesis 2:8-9.* Like the dividing firmament placed "in the midst of the waters" that destroyed the pre-Adamic earth, the tree of life and the tree of knowledge of good and evil were placed in the midst of the garden before Adam and Eve, giving them a choice to remain in faith and follow God, or rebel as Lucifer did. *"But of the tree of the knowledge of good and evil, thou shalt not eat of it: for **in the day** that thou eatest thereof **thou shalt surely die"*** Genesis 2:17. Adam rebelled, and he did die on the day he ate of the fruit as God said he would, for Adam lived 930 years. *"But, beloved, be not ignorant of this one thing, that **one day** is with the Lord as a **thousand years**, and a thousand years as one day"* 2 Peter 3:8. Planet Earth was to become nothing more than a massive graveyard over the next 7,000 years and the journey of life had become the laborious path to death for those without a Savior.

Why was the garden planted eastward in Eden? Eastward is where God's Holy Mountain, the city of Jerusalem resides, *"O Lord, according to all thy righteousness, I beseech thee, let thine anger and thy fury be turned away from thy city **Jerusalem, thy holy mountain:"*** Daniel 9:16. Eastward is where the sun rises every day. Eastward is where God's Son Jesus defeated death and was raised from the grave. Eastward in Eden would be modern-day Iraq, known historically for its abundantly fertile valley, while to the west is Israel. It is the same landmass once appointed to Lucifer (Ezekiel 28) now given to the children of Israel to inherit forever according to God's plan. *"For the LORD shall comfort **Zion**: he will comfort* *all her waste places; and he will make her* **wilderness like Eden,** *and her* **desert like the garden** *of the LORD; joy and gladness shall be found therein, thanksgiving, and the voice of melody" Isaiah 51:3.*

> *"Thus the* **heavens** *and the earth were finished, and all the host of them. And on the seventh day God ended his work which he had* **made;** *and he* **rested** *on the seventh day from all his work which he had* **made.** *And God blessed the seventh day, and sanctified it: because that in it he had rested from all his work which God* **created and made.** *These are the* **generations** *of the* **heavens** *and of the* **earth** *when they were* **created,** *in the day that the LORD God* **made the earth** *and the* **heavens,"** *Genesis 2:1-4.*

Day 7- On the seventh day, God rested from His work and announces the heaven and earth account have now become generations, plural. Generations typify more than one account. The phrase **"And God said Let",** occurs exactly eight times in the KJV, all in Genesis 1. The phrase is mentioned each time God "created" or "made." The biblical number eight represents **new beginnings** as in, *"Which sometime were disobedient, when once the long-suffering of God waited in the days of Noah, while the ark was a preparing, wherein few, that is,* **eight souls were** *saved* by water" *1 Peter 3:20*. God is letting us know in his Word that this seven-day event is a "new beginning" for the Heaven and Earth previously destroyed in Genesis 1:2.

The Lord says he created the Earth not in vain. Why? Because it was in ruins in Genesis 1:2. *"For thus saith the LORD that created the heavens; God himself that **formed the earth** and **made** it; he hath established it, he **created it not in vain**, he formed it to be inhabited: I am the LORD; and **there is none else"** Isaiah 45:18*. God had rescinded Lucifer's authority over the earth and gave it to Adam. *"Ye are blessed of the LORD which **made** heaven and earth. The heaven, even the heavens, are the LORD'S: **but the earth hath he given** to the children of men"* Psalms 115:15-16. The war for the Kingdom rages on.

CHAPTER 2

THE HOST
OF HEAVEN

Darkness is a reminder that we live in a sinful, fallen universe, here to stay until God creates the new heaven and earth. Darkness and light are a clear distinction between good and evil. Most of the universe resides in darkness, while earth has a daily division of day and night. Instinctively, a child may fear and understand that the presence of darkness is not natural to the order of life. Darkness has not always been present. Before Lucifer's fall, Heaven was lit by the host of heaven, that is, the stars, the angels of heaven. Heaven had not yet been divided and stretched until day two of the Genesis renewal event (Isaiah 45:12, Genesis 1:6-8). Perhaps Heaven looked like Vincent van Gogh's *The Starry Night* painting. One could only imagine the magnificence and sparkling grandeur it presented at that time. This division and stretching of

Heaven resulted in our known universe today and was the "big bang" of the evolutionary crowd.

Angels can travel between earth and heaven, but their natural habitat is amongst the stars. A study of "the host of heaven" and "stars of heaven" in the Bible reveals an almost synonymous connection between stars and angels. Some examples follow:

> *"It is he that sitteth upon the circle of the earth, and the inhabitants thereof are as grasshoppers;* **that stretcheth out the heavens as a curtain,** *and spreadeth them out <u>as a tent to dwell in</u>:"*
> Isaiah 40:22

> *"And hath gone and served **other gods,** and worshipped them, either the sun, or moon, or any of the **host of heaven,** which I have not commanded."*
> Deuteronomy 17:3

> *"He telleth the number of the **stars;** he **calleth them** all by **their names.**"*
> Psalms 147:4

> *"Thou, even thou, art LORD alone; thou hast made heaven, the heaven of heavens, with **all their host,** the earth, and all things that are therein, the seas, and all that is therein, and thou preservest them all; and the **host of heaven worshippeth thee.**"*
> Nehemiah 9:6

*"And it waxed great, even to the **host of heaven;** and it **cast down some of the host** and **of the stars** to the ground, and stamped upon them."*
Daniel 8:10

*"And the **stars of heaven shall fall,** and the powers that are in heaven shall be shaken."*
Mark 13:25

*"And his tail drew the third part of **the stars of heaven,** and did cast them to the earth: and the dragon stood before the woman which was ready to be delivered, for to devour her child as soon as it was born."*
Revelation 12:4

*"And the fifth angel sounded, and I saw a **star** fall from heaven unto the earth: and **to him** was given the key of the bottomless pit."*
Revelation 9:1

*"The mystery of the seven stars which thou sawest in my right hand, and the seven golden candlesticks. **The seven stars are the angels** of the seven churches: and the seven candlesticks which thou sawest are the seven churches."*
Revelation 1:20

The Israelites made a counterfeit star representing their god in this telling passage. *"Have ye offered unto me sacrifices and offerings in the wilderness forty years, O house of Israel? But ye have borne the tabernacle of your Moloch and Chiun your images, the **star of your god,** which ye made to yourselves." Amos 5:25-26.*

When the galactic battle came upon Lucifer and his fallen just before Genesis 1:2, sin had tainted all creation. The light of the sun and stars were withheld, and darkness presented itself, engulfing the earth. *"When I made the **cloud the garment** thereof, and **thick darkness** a **swaddlingband** for it," Job 38:9.* The angels shine in the glory given to them by God, but when the Lord presents in wrath and fierce anger, His glory is withheld, and the stars will once again withhold their light when the "Day of the Lord" comes.

> *"Howl ye; for the **day of the LORD** is at hand; it shall come as a destruction from the Almighty. Therefore shall all hands be faint, and every man's heart shall melt: And they shall be afraid: pangs and sorrows shall take hold of them; they shall be in pain as a woman that travaileth: they shall be amazed one at another; their faces shall be as flames. Behold, the day of the LORD cometh, cruel both with **wrath and fierce anger,** to lay the land desolate: and he shall destroy the sinners*

*thereof out of it. For **the stars of heaven and the constellations thereof shall not give their light:** **the sun shall be darkened in his going forth, and the moon shall not cause her light to shine.** And I will punish the world for their evil, and the wicked for their iniquity; and I will cause the arrogancy of the proud to cease, and will lay low the haughtiness **of the terrible.***"
Isaiah 13:6-11.

"*The sun and the moon shall be darkened, and the **stars shall withdraw their shining.***"
Joel 3:15

"*And, lo, **the angel** of the Lord came upon them, and the **glory of the Lord shone** round about them: and they were sore afraid.*"
Luke 2:9

"*And after these things I saw another **angel** come down from heaven, having great power; and **the earth was lightened with his glory.***"
Revelation 18:1

"*There is one glory of the sun, and another glory of the moon, and **another glory of the stars:** for **one star differeth from another star in glory.***"
1 Corinthians 15:41

The angels differ in glory depending on their rank. The more powerful angels/stars will shine much brighter than those of a lesser rank. Interestingly, the astronomical community has given a stellar classification to stars, meaning stars are classified into types according to their temperatures as estimated from their spectra or color of light. This ranking consists of seven types, from hot to cool stars. The order of stellar types is O, B, A, F, G, K, M; our sun is ranked a G. Also interesting are the seven ranks, for seven in biblical terms represents God's program on behalf of man.

God had charged some of His angels with folly. Did the angels that sinned with Lucifer have their habitat star turn into a neutron star or, similarly, a star experiencing an internal explosion causing the core to collapse within itself, extinguishing its light?

> *"Behold, he put **no trust** in his **servants**; and his **angels** he charged with **folly**:"*
> *Job 4:18*

> *"Behold, he putteth **no trust** in his **saints**; yea, the **heavens are not clean** in his sight."*
> *Job 15:15.*

> *"Behold even to the **moon, and it shineth not**; yea, the **stars are not pure in his sight**."*
> *Job 15:15*

The sinning angels charged with folly were disembodied and turned into wandering spirits. Without a natural body, they became wandering stars, evil spirits, to be cast into the lake of fire with darkness forever. "Raging waves of the sea, foaming out their own shame; *wandering stars*, to whom is *reserved the blackness of darkness for ever*" Jude 1:13.

Only God can provide a spirit, the breath of life, and when an angel's body is destroyed, his spirit "wanders" looking for a host. Man's spirit upon death returns to God, who gave it. *"Who knoweth the **spirit of man that goeth upward**, and the spirit of the beast that goeth downward to the earth?" Ecclesiastes 3:21.* If at death the man was saved in Jesus, his spirit will be reunited with his soul as a spiritual body at the resurrection. *"It is sown a natural body; it is **raised a spiritual body**. There is a natural body, and there is a spiritual body" 1 Corinthians 15:44.*

The Lord's righteous angels are his ministers. *"Bless the LORD, **ye his angels**, that excel in strength, that **do his commandments**, hearkening unto the voice of his word. Bless ye the LORD, all ye his hosts; **ye ministers of his, that do his pleasure**" Psalms 103:20-21.* An angel can have multiple functions as a minister of the Lord. They can be warriors, messengers, protectors, comforters, etc.

The popular view today is that demons are the disembodied spirits of the giants wiped out in Noah's flood. Or could it be they are the wandering stars of Jude?

"By the word of the LORD were the heavens made; and all the host of them by the breath of his mouth."
Psalm 33:6

"The Spirit of God hath made me, and the breath of the Almighty hath given me life."
Job 33:4

The preceding two verses show that God breathes life into all living beings. His breath is life and instills the spirit into the body. Only God can give a spirit and true life.

"Thus saith God the LORD, he that created the heavens, and stretched them out; he that spread forth the earth, and that which cometh out of it; he that giveth breath unto the people upon it, and spirit to them that walk therein:"
Isaiah 42:5

"All the while my breath is in me, and the spirit of God is in my nostrils;"
Job 27:3

"And the LORD God formed man of the dust of the ground, and breathed into his nostrils the breath of life; and man became a living soul."
Genesis 2:7

*"Then shall the dust return to the earth as it was: and the **spirit** shall **return unto God who gave it**."*
Ecclesiastes 2:7

The giants were produced in rebellion by angels mating with humans. *"There were **giants** in the earth in those days; and also after that, when the **sons of God** came in unto the **daughters of men**, and **they bare children to them**, the same became mighty men which were of old, men of renown"* *Genesis 6:4*. These angels were another group of fallen angels from Genesis 6, and not part of the original rebelling angels of Lucifer's hoard. The giants they produced as offspring were alive, but they had not the breath of life, a living spirit, for if they did, God would have instructed Noah to load them into the ark. *"And they went in unto Noah into the ark, two and two of all flesh, **wherein is the breath of life**"* *Genesis 7:15*.

The demons are called unclean spirits and devils in the New Testament. They are the same, however there is a distinct division between angels and spirits. A fully intact angel has flesh and bone, while a spirit, or disembodied angel, does not.

*"Behold my hands and my feet, that it is I myself: handle me, and see; for a **spirit hath not flesh and bones**, as ye see me have."*
Luke 24:39

*"And as he was yet a coming, the **devil** threw him down, and tare him. And Jesus rebuked the **unclean spirit**, and healed the child, and delivered him again to his father."*
Luke 9:42

*"And I saw three **unclean spirits** like frogs come out of the **mouth of the dragon**, and out of the **mouth of the beast**, and out of the mouth of the **false prophet**. For **they are the spirits of devils**, working miracles, which go forth unto the kings of the earth and of the whole world, to gather them to the battle of that great day of God Almighty."*
Revelation 16:13-14

*"And there arose a great cry: and the scribes that were of the Pharisees' part arose, and strove, saying, We find no evil in this man: but if a **spirit or an angel** hath spoken to him, let us not fight against God."*
Acts 23:9

The devils/unclean spirits knew Jesus from the time of their creation as they stood before his presence many times. During their encounters with Jesus on earth, the Lord prohibited them from speaking freely of His identity. *"And **unclean spirits**, when they saw him, **fell down before him**, and cried, saying, Thou art the Son of God.*

*And he straitly charged them that **they should not make him known*** Mark 3:11-12. "*And he healed many that were sick of divers diseases, and cast out many **devils**; and **suffered not the devils to speak**, because they knew him*" *Mark 1:34.*

Devils, unclean spirits, and gods are the same. In the Old Testament, these demons were called gods. God himself also called the fallen angels gods.

> *"They sacrificed unto **devils**, not to God; to **gods** whom they knew not, to new gods that came newly up, whom your fathers feared not."*
> *Deuteronomy 32:17*

> *"God standeth in the **congregation** of the mighty; he judgeth among the **gods**., I have said, **Ye are gods**; and all of you are **children** of the most High. But **ye shall die like men**, and fall like one of the princes. Arise, O God, judge the earth: for **thou shalt inherit all nations (war for the Kingdom)**."*
> *Psalm 82:1, 6-8*

Beelzebub was the Jewish name for Satan. The scribes accused Jesus of casting out devils by Satan, but Jesus rebuked them, charged them with blasphemy, and used the words "unclean spirit" in place of "devils."

> *"And the scribes which came down from Jerusalem said, **He hath Beelzebub**, and by the **prince of the***

devils casteth he out devils. "
Mark 3:22

*"But he that shall blaspheme against the Holy
Ghost hath never forgiveness, but is in danger of
eternal damnation: Because they said, He hath an
unclean spirit."*
Mark 3:29-30

Finally, Jude's wandering stars (1:13) are demons that
cannot rest, that are continually **"foaming out their own
shame"** in a rage. Foaming at the mouth is associated with
rage. A horse will foam at the mouth when enraged.

*"And one of the multitude answered and said,
Master, I have brought unto thee my son, which
hath a dumb spirit; And wheresoever he taketh
him, he teareth him: and he foameth, and gnasheth
with his teeth, and pineth away: and I spake to
thy disciples that they should cast him out; and
they could not. He answereth him, and saith,
O faithless generation, how long shall I be with
you? how long shall I suffer you? bring him unto
me. And they brought him unto him: and when he
saw him, straightway the spirit tare him; and he
fell on the ground, and wallowed foaming."*
Mark 9:17-20

Could it be demons do not like water, as it's how these fallen angels had their bodies destroyed and their spirit disembodied by the destructive waters of the deep in Genesis 1:2? Hence, the sea above the firmament keeps them out unless God calls an assembly granting them passage. These evil spirits have different levels of wickedness and seek rest within the human body. The unclean spirit is referred to as "he" "himself," as in a male, for there are no female angels.

> *"When the **unclean spirit** is gone out of a man, he walketh through **dry places, seeking rest**, and findeth none. Then he saith, I will return into my house from whence I came out; and when he is come, he findeth it empty, swept, and garnished. Then goeth he, and taketh with himself **seven other spirits more wicked than himself**, and they enter in and dwell there:"*
> *Mattew 12:43-45*

> *"Saying to the sixth angel which had the trumpet, Loose the four **angels** which are **bound** in the great **river** Euphrates."*
> *Revelation 9:14*

Not all fallen angels rebelled at the same time that Lucifer sinned. However, at the time of the birth of Jesus, ⅓ of the angels had sided with Satan. The rebelling angels of

Genesis 6 are chained in the lower part of hell, sucked down by the receding waters of Noah's flood. The others are still in our presence.

> *"And the angels which **kept not their first estate**, but left their own habitation, he hath **reserved in everlasting chains** under darkness unto the **judgment of the great day**."*
> Jude 1:6

> *"And **his tail drew the third part of the stars of heaven**, and did cast them to the earth: and the dragon stood before the woman which was ready to be delivered, **for to devour her child as soon as it was born**."*
> Revelation 12:4.

CHAPTER 3

LUCIFER

In the beginning God created the heaven and the earth.
Genesis 1:1

At some point long ago, God created a family of souls, some of them in his image, to establish a community and fellowship, to form a kingdom. He created various forms of sentient life to inhabit Heaven. These included the angels innumerable, cherubim, seraphim, and other cosmic creatures. Using their intellect, they were able to choose their path. They could contribute to God's holy plan or reject it in a desire to direct their own path from the newly formed kingdom and the face of God. They would have to choose between good and evil. They existed in harmony with the Father in a relationship of trust and faith in his infinite wisdom and sovereignty of life in the kingdom.

As these beings matured, God chose to create the first planet, Earth. Perhaps the entirety was like the Garden of Eden, a magnificent display of His glory. Here, God would place creatures of all sorts not made in his image: those that fly, swim, crawl, and walk. It would also include trees of all sorts, including the nut and fruit-bearing kind, and many types of seed-bearing grasses to feed all of the creatures. He would give the new planet its own star—the sun—for warmth and the energy of life, allowing the plants to flourish. As the foundations of Earth were laid, the morning stars (angels) shouted for joy to see the creation as it was created. Upon its completion, Lucifer the cherub was appointed potentate of this new planet. Yet sometime after, the newly-created planet would lie in ruins.

> *"Where wast thou when **I laid the foundations of the earth**? declare, if thou hast understanding."*
> *Job 38:4*

> *"**Of old hast thou laid the foundation** of the earth: and the heavens are the work of thy hands."*
> *Psalms 102:25*

> *"When the **morning stars sang** together, and all the **sons of God shouted for joy**?"*
> *Job 38:7*

If you ask people the question, "Who was the first murderer," most will say incorrectly, "Cain," who slayed his brother Abel. But Lucifer was the first sinner, a murderer from the beginning. He is the father of lies, the first liar. Hence, it is why the tree of knowledge of good and evil was present in the garden *before* Adam sinned, and the *purpose* for which Jesus was made manifest: to destroy the works of the Devil. Many Christians do not understand that Hell, was not created for man, but for the Devil and his angels. Think about this for a minute: Lucifer, the first murderer, produced the power of death. In this life, death is the ultimate, unfortunate destiny for all living on this planet.

> *"Ye are of your father the Devil, and the lusts of your father ye will do. He was a **murderer from the beginning**, and abode not in the truth, because there is no truth in him. When he speaketh a lie, he speaketh of his own: for **he is a liar, and the father of it.**"*
> *John 8:44*

> *"He that committeth sin is of the Devil; for the devil sinneth from the beginning. **For this purpose the Son of God was manifested**, that he might destroy the works of the Devil."*
> *1 John 3:8*

> *"Forasmuch then as the **children are partakers of flesh and blood,** he also himself likewise took*

*part of the same; that **through death he might
destroy him** that had the **power of death**, that is,
the **Devil**;"*
Hebrews 2:14

*"Then shall he say also unto them on the left
hand, Depart from me, ye cursed, into everlasting
fire, **prepared for the Devil and his angels**:"*
Matthew 25:41

*"And **death and hell** were **cast** into the **lake of
fire**. This is the second death."*
Revelation 20:14

Sin was already within the creation when God said, "The
man is become as one of us," meaning man now under-
stood as God and the heavenly beings already did: to
know good and evil. *"And the LORD God said, Behold,
the **man is become** as one of **us**, to **know good and evil**:
and now, lest he put forth his hand, and take also of the
tree of life, and eat, and live for ever:"* Genesis 3:22. Who
did Lucifer murder and what was his first lie? We are not
given the answer to those questions, but *"The thing that
hath been, it is that which shall be; and that which is done
is that which shall be done: and **there is no new thing
under the sun**"* Ecclesiastes 1:9. Perhaps Lucifer murdered
a fellow cherub as Cain slayed his brother Abel. Perhaps
Lucifer, as a traitor, betrayed God just as Judas betrayed

Jesus. Regardless, Lucifer's sin would soon lead to catastrophic consequences: war with the Lord of Host, the loss of his celestial body, and the destruction of the new planet Earth. Ezekiel 28 describes much of what we know about Lucifer.

> *"Son of man, take up a lamentation upon the king of Tyrus, and say unto him, Thus saith the Lord GOD; Thou **sealest up the sum**, full of wisdom, and perfect in beauty."*
> *Ezekiel 28:12*

Lucifer was the most perfect being God created. He was heir to planet Earth, with his home base in Eden. He was responsible as worship leader of the angelic beings to bring glory, gratitude, honor, and praise to God. It is important to note that Lucifer was not created in the likeness and image of God as the angels and men were, for he was a cherub, one of five cherubs assigned to the throne of the One that possesses Heaven and Earth. Four cherubs transported the throne while Lucifer was the "anointed cherub that covereth." As a king is anointed to protect and legislate his domain, Lucifer held the highest position under his Creator. In time, however, God's kingdom was threatened from within. God cast out Lucifer and his rebels, destroyed the earth, and replaced the sinning Lucifer with Adam as the crown jewel of His creation. It enraged Lucifer that his dominion was given to a lesser being. Emotionally unable to handle this change of dominion, he set out to battle with the support of his cohorts against this renewing of the earth and God's plan for man. Lucifer succeeded in deceiving Eve to eat the forbidden fruit. Adam chose to follow his wife and sinned with her, allowing Satan to regain dominion of Earth. Satan continues his battle today (Ephesians 6:12), but in the end, Earth will be returned to man. *"The heaven, even the heavens, are the LORD'S: **but the earth hath he given to the children of men**" Psalms 115:16.*

> *"**Thou hast been in Eden** the garden of God; every **precious stone was thy covering**, the sardius, topaz, and the diamond, the beryl, the onyx, and the jasper, the sapphire, the emerald, and the carbuncle, and gold: the workmanship of **thy tabrets** and of **thy pipes** was prepared in thee in the day that thou wast created."*
> *Ezekiel 28:13*

Lucifer had these precious stones as a covering for at least two reasons. Lucifer's name means light-bearer, shining one, the morning star. These stones once magnificently reflected the glory of God. As the "anointed cherub that covereth," Lucifer displayed an array of light when covering the throne of God and as heir of the earth before his fall. Of the nine stones mentioned in Ezekiel 28:13, eight are anisotropic; the diamond is isotropic. Gold can be either one, depending on its structure.

Under a microscope, if a ray of light is passed through an anisotropic stone, the stone will break down the light inside the stone and propagate it with two different refractive light rays bursting into a glorious pattern of rainbow colors. Conversely, the isotropic stone (diamond) will only produce darkness, hence the stones of Lucifer produced light. This is how all of God's light-bearing angelic hosts can produce light by reflecting His Glory. *"And after these things I saw another angel come down from heaven, having great power; and **the earth was lightened with his glory**" Revelation 18:1.*

> *"Thou art the **anointed cherub** that **covereth**; and I have **set thee so**: thou wast upon the **holy mountain of God**; thou hast **walked up and down** in the midst of the **stones of fire**"*
> *Ezekiel 28:14.*

During Lucifer's reign, access to God's holy mountain was present on Earth/Eden, perhaps from within the garden. There was no divide between God's abode and His creation. God's family all lived in unison. Lucifer had complete access as he was **"set"** over the creation. At the base of the mountain going upward to God's throne were the stones of fire. Stones like those embedded within Lucifer lit up the holy mountain in majestic splendor. When all enemies are defeated, God will return to dwell again among His creation, and the new city of Jerusalem will contain these precious stones to display and reflect the glory of God.

> *"And I John saw the holy city, new Jerusalem, coming down from God out of heaven, prepared as a bride adorned for her husband. And I heard a great voice out of heaven saying, Behold, the tabernacle of God is with men, and **he will dwell with them**, and they shall be his people, and God himself shall be with them, and be their God."*
> Revelation 21:2-3

> *"And he carried me away in the spirit to a great and high mountain, and shewed me that great city, the holy Jerusalem, descending out of heaven from God, Having the **glory of God: and her light was like unto a stone most precious,** even like a jasper stone, clear as crystal;"*
> Revelation 21:10-11

> *"And **the foundations** of the wall of the city were **garnished with all manner of precious stones.** The first foundation was jasper; the second, sapphire; the third, a chalcedony; the fourth, an emerald; The fifth, sardonyx; the sixth, sardius; the*

*seventh, chrysolite; the eighth, beryl; the ninth, a topaz; the tenth, a chrysoprasus; the eleventh, a jacinth; the twelfth, an amethyst. And **the city had no need of the sun**, neither of the moon, to shine in it: for the **glory of God did lighten it**, and the Lamb is the light thereof."*
Revelation 21:19-20, 23

The last stone of Lucifer's covering is not a stone, but rather the mineral, gold. This brings us to the second reason for the stones of Lucifer. The stones and gold are how Lucifer obtained his "power" as protector and guardian. Light is energy and can be used in various number of ways. Many connections between electricity, lightning, and the spirit world cannot be written within the context of this book. Quartz stones produce an electrical current when squeezed and vibrate when electrified. Perhaps this is how Lucifer activated the tabrets and pipes in his body to produce music in his priestly role as the worship leader of the angelic realm in his sanctuaries. These stones are very efficient at conducting electricity, while gold is the most reliable and durable conductor. Quartz and gold are used in most electronic devices today. The high priest's breastplate of the Old Testament held 12 of these precious stones connected to "wires" attached to the plates of gold. The streets of the new city of Jerusalem will be paved in gold, radiating with the flow of God's energy. Man to this day, still does not fully understand the complexity and source of electricity.

> "And they did **beat the gold into thin plates,** and cut it into **wires,** to work it in the blue, and in the purple, and in the scarlet, and in the fine linen, with cunning work."
> Exodus 39:3

> "And the twelve gates were twelve pearls; every several gate was of one pearl: and the **street of the city was pure gold,** as it were transparent glass."
> Revelation 21:21

As one that "covereth," Lucifer was more powerful than all other celestial beings. In the Bible, fire is often associated with lightning. Making note of his immense power, Jesus said, "I beheld Satan as lightning," immediately after the apostles returned, celebrating their success in casting out devils. Jesus had granted the apostles, via His name, the power of deliverance from Satan's minions, and to show how powerful Satan was, described him as lightning. Falling from Heaven at the speed of light must have plunged Lucifer to a great depth within the Earth. Was this when Hell was created? The Antichrist obtains his "power" from the dragon (Satan), and he will honor the "God of forces."

> "And the seventy returned again with joy, saying, Lord, even the devils are subject unto us through

thy name. And he said unto them, I beheld Satan as lightning fall from heaven."
Luke 10:17-18

"And they worshipped the dragon which gave power unto the beast: and they worshipped the beast, saying, Who is like unto the beast? who is able to make war with him?"
Revelation 13:4

"And he doeth great wonders, so that he maketh fire come down from heaven on the earth in the sight of men."
Revelation 13:13

"But in his estate shall he honour the God of forces: and a god whom his fathers knew not shall he honour with gold, and silver, and with precious stones, and pleasant things"
Daniel 11:38

It is these same stones that empower the four cherubim who carry God's chariot of fire. God is the "force" of all creation and from him is given *"power"* to whom he wills. All matter is a form of energy, and all energy belongs to God. At certain times, the Lord is pictured in his power of fire and lightning.

"As for the likeness of the living creatures, their appearance was like burning coals of fire, and

*like the appearance of lamps: it went up and down among the living creatures; and the fire was bright, and **out of the fire went forth lightning.** And the living creatures ran and returned as the appearance of a **flash of lightning***".
Ezekiel 1:13-14

*"God hath spoken once; twice have I heard this; that **power belongeth unto God.**"*
Psalms 62:11

*"And above the firmament that was over their heads was the likeness of a throne, as the appearance of a **sapphire stone**: and upon the likeness of the Throne was the likeness as the appearance of a man above upon it. And I saw as the colour of amber, as the **appearance of fire round about within it, from the appearance of his loins even upward, and from the appearance of his loins even downward, I saw as it were the appearance of fire,** and it had brightness round about."*
Ezekiel 1:26-27

*"For as the **lightning** cometh out of the east, and shineth even unto the west; so shall also **the coming of the Son of man be.**"*
Matthew 24:27 (Rapture of the church).

*"And, behold, there was a great earthquake: for the **angel of the Lord** descended from heaven, and came and rolled back the stone from the door, and sat upon it. His **countenance was like lightning**, and his raiment white as snow:"*
Matthew 28:2-3 (at the resurrection of Jesus, the glory of this angel represented the glory of Christ).

Back to Ezekiel chapter 28:

*"Thou wast perfect in thy ways from the day that thou wast created, **till iniquity** was found in thee. By the multitude of thy **merchandise** they have filled the midst of thee with **violence**, and thou hast **sinned**: therefore I will **cast thee as profane** out of the mountain of God: and I will **destroy thee**, O covering cherub, **from the midst of the stones of fire."***
Ezekiel 28:15-16

Though Scripture does not tell us how long it was from Lucifer's creation until he sinned, it seems that it was a short time. *"**For the love of money is the root of all evil**: which while some coveted after, they have **erred from the faith**, and pierced themselves through with many sorrows"* 1 Timothy 6:10. Not money, but the love of money is the root of all evil. The holder is apt to gain dominance, prestige, riches, influence, and a sense of respect based on fear given by others under the influence of the holder. Somehow, Lucifer, the angels, and other heavenly beings were dealing in merchandising, trafficking, and trade to the point of profane indulgence that eventually led to violence. Lucifer had abandoned his trust in God's plan and direction that was set before him. Having failed in his faith towards God, Lucifer could only trust in the wickedness of his pride, and as a result, Jesus saw Lucifer cast out as profane from the mountain of God. *"And he said unto them, I beheld Satan as lightning fall from heaven"* *Luke 10:18.*

No longer holy, the most beautiful creature of creation had his **body destroyed** and lost access to the gateway of God's holy mountain, for God formed him into the winding, crooked serpent, the one that plays in the sea. *"By his spirit, he hath garnished the heavens; his hand hath formed the crooked serpent"* *Job 26:13.* *"There go the ships: there is that leviathan, whom thou hast made to play therein"* *Psalms 104:26.* Lucifer had become "the dragon, that old serpent." Why a sea serpent? Why a dragon? Like all cherubs, Lucifer has four faces and four wings. The ox is his natural face and represents all domesticated mammals; the other three include a man's face for mankind, the lion representing all predator mammals, and the eagle representing all fowl. None of them represent the enormous **dinosaur reptile kingdom.** Note that Jesus, the lion of Judah, stands at the right hand of God, as does the cherub's lion face, while the ox, the natural face of the cherub, resides on the left side of the face.

> *"As for the likeness of their faces, they four had the face of a man, and the face of a lion, on the right side: and they four had the face of an **ox** on the **left side**; they four also had the face of an eagle."*
> *Ezekiel 1:10*

> *"And every one had four faces: the **first face was the face of a cherub**, and the second face was the face of a man, and the third the face of a lion, and the fourth the face of an eagle."*
> *Ezekiel 10:14*

During his reign of Earth, Lucifer and the fallen angels corrupted the original animals, reptiles, and plant life God had created, for he wanted to be "like God." Many of these animals were probably much different than what we see today. For example, the unicorn is mentioned six times in the Bible, and the celestial flying horse is used to carry Elijah into heaven and the saints back with Jesus. In his corruption of the mammal, specifically the reptile kingdom, Lucifer manipulated the dinosaurs and other beastly creatures and became King of the Reptiles. Some of these dinosaurs looked vicious and deformed, not within the nature of a Holy God. Some were meat eaters. God had given all beast and man the herb to eat before the flood of Noah. It was only after Noah's flood that God gave meat to be eaten, placing the time of the dinosaurs before man.

> *"And God said, Behold, I have given you **every herb** bearing seed, which is upon the face of all the earth, and every tree, in the which is the **fruit** of a tree yielding seed; to you it **shall be for meat.**"*
> *Genesis 1:29*

> *"And to **every beast of the earth,** and to **every fowl** of the air, and to **every thing that creepeth** upon the earth, wherein there is life, I have given **every green herb for meat:** and it was so."*
> *Genesis 1:30*

> *"**Every moving thing that liveth shall be meat** for you; even as the green herb have I given you all things."*
> *Genesis 9:3*

Many of the gods and monsters of ancient mythological lore were reptilian in nature, and today's occult uses the reptilian image within their domain. Unlike any other creature, the dragon resides at the top of the animal chain. Dragons are known and imbedded in every culture on the earth. Not only is the dragon a reptile who abodes in the sea but also a serpentine type of flying beast, for Lucifer the cherub had hooved feet.

*"And their feet were straight feet; and the **sole of their feet was like the sole of a calf's foot**: and they sparkled like the colour of burnished brass."*
Ezekiel 1:7

*"Canst thou bind the **unicorn** with his band in the furrow? or will he harrow the valleys after thee?"*
Job 39:10

*"And it came to pass, as they still went on, and talked, that, behold, there appeared a chariot of fire, and **horses of fire**, and parted them both asunder; and Elijah went up by a whirlwind into heaven."*
2 Kings 2:11

*"And the armies which were in heaven **followed him upon white horses**, clothed in fine linen, white and clean."*
Revelation 19:14

Lucifer shone the brightest among the beings that displayed the light of God's glory. His beauty, wisdom, and superiority over the earth blinded him into thinking he was equal to or stronger than God, and rightfully the one that should reside on the Throne. However, Satan, as powerful as he may be, is still a created being from God, and any attempt against God will be futile. *"**Pride** goeth before* *destruction, and an* **haughty spirit** *before a fall" Proverbs 16:18.*

> *"Thine heart was lifted up because of thy beauty,* ***thou hast corrupted thy wisdom by reason of thy brightness:*** *I will* ***cast thee to the ground,*** *I will lay thee before kings, that they may behold thee. Thou hast* ***defiled thy sanctuaries by the multitude of thine iniquities, by the iniquity*** *of thy* ***traffick;*** *therefore will I bring forth a fire from the midst of thee, it shall devour thee, and I will* ***bring thee to ashes upon the earth in the sight of all them that behold thee."***
> *Ezekiel 28:17-18*

From the preceding verses, one can infer that instead of using his sanctuaries to bring glory to God; Lucifer eventually used them in a defiled way by demanding worship of himself and using the sanctuaries to deal in traffic as a "den of thieves" just like Jesus accused the Jews of his day.

> *And they come to Jerusalem: and Jesus went into the temple, and began to* ***cast out them that sold and bought in the temple,*** *and overthrew the tables of the moneychangers, and the seats of them that sold doves; And would not suffer that any man* ***should carry any vessel through the temple.*** *And he taught, saying unto them, Is it not*

*written, My house shall be called of all nations the house of prayer? but ye have made it a **den of thieves**. Mark 11:15-17*

Satan will be cast to the ground from Heaven at the mid-point of the Tribulation, no longer able to roam the solar system or be "called" into the presence of God for an assembly. *"And the great dragon was cast out, that old serpent, called the Devil, and Satan, which deceiveth the whole world: he was **cast out into the earth**, and his angels were cast out with him" Revelation 12:9.* Satan will be devoured by fire and **brought to ashes** at the end of the Millennial Rein.

> *"And when the **thousand years** are expired, **Satan** shall be loosed out of his prison, And shall go out to deceive the nations which are in the four quarters of the earth, Gog and Magog, to gather them together to battle: the number of whom is as the sand of the sea. And **they went up** on the breadth of the earth, and **compassed the camp of the saints** about, and the beloved city: and **fire came down from God out of heaven, and devoured them.**"* Revelation 20:7-9

Understanding the meaning of biblical numbers is vital to gaining a deeper discernment of the scriptures. The biblical number four represents something whole in structure or nature. For example, the new city of Jerusalem will be foursquare, making a complete and perfect cube (Revelation 21:16). The original number four, as written, looked similar to the "+" symbol before our modern day "4". The + expressed the four directions of N, S, E, and W, the four winds of Earth (Revelation 7:1). Its relationship to the cross of Christ solidifies the understanding of wholeness. The DNA of all living things consists of four letters, the four bases found in a DNA molecule, ACGT. In the four chambers of the human heart, the four states of matter are solid, liquid, gas, and plasma.

Lucifer is "cast" out and down a total of four times. The first "cast," along with losing his celestial body, happened sometime in the ancient past, while the last three are yet future. He was:

1. Cast out of the holy mountain of God (Ezekiel 28:16).
2. Cast out of Heaven permanently, Revelation 12:9.
3. Cast into the bottomless pit, Revelation 20:3.
4. Cast into the lake of fire and brimstone, Revelation 20:10, completing the wholeness of the battle for the Kingdom.

Now, we shall turn our attention to Isaiah chapter 14.

"How art thou fallen from heaven, O Lucifer, son of the morning! how art thou cut down to

the ground, which didst weaken the nations! For thou hast said in thine heart, I will ascend into heaven, I will exalt my Throne above the stars of God: I will sit also upon the mount of the congregation, in the sides of the north: I will ascend above the heights of the clouds; I will be like the most High."
Isaiah 14:12-14

In the passage above are the infamous five "I will" statements of doom by Lucifer. God responded to each of Lucifer's five statements in striking symmetry with his own five "I will" statements of judgment covered previously in Ezekiel 28:16-18. The book of Isaiah was written **before** Ezekiel.

By the multitude of thy merchandise they have filled the midst of thee with violence, and thou hast sinned: therefore I will cast thee as profane out of the mountain of God: and I will destroy thee, O covering cherub, from the midst of the stones of fire. Thine heart was lifted up because of thy beauty, thou hast corrupted thy wisdom by reason of thy brightness: I will cast thee to the ground, I will lay thee before kings, that they may behold thee. Thou hast defiled thy sanctuaries by the multitude of thine iniquities, by the iniquity

of thy traffick; therefore will I bring forth a fire
*from the midst of thee, it shall devour thee, and **I***
***will** bring thee to ashes upon the earth in the sight*
of all them that behold thee."
Ezekiel 28:16-18

Lucifer did not have supreme authority over God's angels, nor was he satisfied with his earthly throne as the anointed one, worship leader, and guardian of God's throne. At some point early in his reign, he desired to move his throne into heaven above the stars, above the angels of God. He desired to sit as leader of the congregation, the assembly God ordered of the holy community of angels and other celestial beings that was "in the sides of the north" on Mount Zion. *"Great is the LORD, and greatly to be praised in the **city of our God**, in the mountain of his holiness. Beautiful for situation, the joy of the whole earth, **is mount Zion, on the sides of the north**, the **city** of the great **King**"* Psalms 48:1-2. Had Lucifer not sinned, he would still be the worship leader today, bringing honor, glory, and praise to God. As the "heights of the clouds" testify, his throne was on the earth. Still, he desired to be like the "most High," the one that would call for the assembly of the holy ones.

*"Yet thou shalt be **brought down to hell**, to the*
sides of the pit. They that see thee shall narrowly

look upon thee, and consider thee, saying, Is this
the man *that made the earth to tremble, that
did shake kingdoms; That* ***made the world as a
wilderness,*** *and* ***destroyed the cities*** *thereof; that*
opened not the house of his prisoners?"
Isaiah 14:15-17.

As Revelation 20:3 also declares, Satan will be cast down
into Hell, the pit. The powerful oppressor is made a spec-
tacle, and those who see him in Hell will be amazed at how
the one that caused so much havoc and destruction on the
earth is now in Hell. As a murderer from the beginning,
he certainly would have held a house of prisoners. In this
context, "house" refers to a family of ancestors, kindred,
or a race of persons from the same stock. Remember, he
was cast out as "profane." What was he trafficking? What
was his "merchandise?" There is nothing new under the
sun. As in Isaiah above, Jeremiah mentions again the
wilderness and destruction of cities.

"***I beheld the earth, and, lo, it was without form,
and void;*** *and the heavens, and* ***they had no light.***
*I beheld the mountains, and, lo, they trembled,
and all the hills moved lightly. I beheld, and, lo,*
there was no man, *and all the birds of the heavens were fled. I beheld, and, lo, the fruitful place
was a* ***wilderness,*** *and all the* ***cities thereof were***

broken down at the presence of the LORD, and
by his fierce anger. For thus hath the LORD said,
The whole land shall be desolate; yet will I not
make a full end."
Jeremiah 4:23-27

The prophet Jeremiah is given a glimpse of the destruction brought by the Lord from the galactic battle that ensued between good and evil. Jeremiah saw the earth as it was in Genesis 1:2, "without form and void." He saw the light of the heavens were taken away, and the earth was empty of life, the "birds of the heavens were fled," and "there was no man." There has not been a time on earth since the creation of Adam that man has not dwelled on it.

Psalm 89 is a very telling theme of the war for the Kingdom. The Lord praises David, his newfound anointed servant. However, after praising David, the tone drastically changes to a negative view of him. Bible Commentaries have trouble explaining this shift in the Lord's tone towards David. Is David really receiving extreme condemnation, or did the Lord suddenly shift to a past or future event as he so often does in the scriptures? Let's look at verses 19-37.

"Then thou spakest in vision to thy holy one, and
saidst, I have laid help upon one that is mighty;
I have exalted one chosen out of the people. I
have found David my servant; with my holy oil
have I anointed him: With whom my hand shall

be established: mine arm also shall strengthen him. **The enemy shall not exact upon him; nor the son of wickedness afflict him.** *And I will* **beat down his foes** *before his face, and* **plague them that hate him.** *But* **my faithfulness and my mercy shall be with him:** *and* **in my name shall his horn be exalted.** *I will set his hand also in the sea, and his right hand in the rivers. He shall cry unto me, Thou art my father, my God, and the rock of my salvation. Also I will make him my firstborn, higher than the kings of the earth.* **My mercy will I keep** *for him* **for evermore,** *and* **my covenant shall stand fast with him.** *His seed also will I make to endure for ever, and his Throne as the days of heaven. If his children forsake my law, and walk not in my judgments; If they break my statutes, and keep not my commandments; Then will I visit their transgression with the rod, and their iniquity with stripes. Nevertheless* **my lovingkindness will I not utterly take from him,** *nor suffer my faithfulness to fail.* **My covenant will I not break,** *nor alter the thing that is gone out of my lips.* **Once have I sworn by my holiness that I will not lie unto David.** *His seed shall endure for ever, and his Throne as the sun before me. It shall be established for ever as the moon, and as a faithful witness in heaven. Selah."*
Psalms 89:19-37

The Lord's strong language of promises to David is clearly outlined in the above. The text will now take a sudden shift with a tone of condemnation. It is the opinion of this author that the Lord is looking back on the pre-Adamic past to the now-fallen Lucifer, who was at one time his anointed. Replacing David with Lucifer suddenly allows the scriptures to make sense, for what the scripture in Acts says of David could never be said of Lucifer. *"And when he had removed him, he raised up unto them David to be their king; to whom also **he gave testimony**, and said, I have **found David** the son of Jesse, **a man after mine own heart**, which shall **fulfil all my will"** Acts 13:22.* Lucifer did not fulfil God's will and was only after the desire of his own heart.

> *"But thou hast cast off and **abhorred, thou hast been wroth with thine anointed.** (abhorred, hated. Did God really hate David?) **Thou hast made void the covenant of thy servant:** thou hast profaned his crown by casting it to the ground. (cast thee as profane out of the mountain of God, Ez.28:16) Thou hast broken down all his hedges; thou hast brought his strong holds to ruin. All that pass by the way spoil him: he is a reproach to his neighbours. Thou hast set up the right hand of his adversaries; **thou hast made all his enemies to rejoice.** (Right hand refers to Jesus) Thou hast*

*also turned the edge of his sword, and hast not made him to stand in the battle (Holy angels and specifically the church, Luke 10:18-19). Thou hast **made his glory to cease,** and cast his Throne down to the ground (Lucifer would no longer reflect God's Glory). The **days of his youth hast thou shortened:** (no longer has eternal life, Rev. 20:10) thou hast **covered him with shame.** (He was made the crooked serpent, Job 26:13, fallen angels foam out their shame, Jude 1:13) Selah."*
Psalm 89:38-45

The beginning of Psalm 89 refers to the Lord's mercies and faithfulness as outlined by the Psalmist in verse 1. The Lord speaks in verses 2-4 on how it shall be done through his servant David.

*"I will sing of the **mercies** of the LORD for ever: with my mouth will I make known thy **faithfulness** to all generations. For I have said, Mercy shall be built up for ever: thy faithfulness shalt thou establish in the very heavens. I have made a **covenant** with **my chosen,** I have **sworn** unto **David** my **servant,** Thy seed will I **establish for ever,** and build up thy Throne to **all generations.** Selah."*
Psalms 89:1-4.

The Psalmist picks back up in verses 5-10.

> *And the* **heavens** *shall praise thy wonders, O LORD: thy faithfulness also in the* **congregation of the saints.** *For* **who in the heaven** *can be* **compared** *unto the LORD? who among the* **sons of the mighty** *can be likened unto the LORD? God is* **greatly to be feared in the assembly of the saints,** *and to be had in reverence of all them that are about him. O* **LORD God of hosts, who is a strong LORD like unto thee?** *or to* **thy faithfulness** *round about thee?* **Thou rulest the raging of the sea:** *when the waves thereof arise, thou stillest them. Thou hast broken* **Rahab** *in pieces, as one that is slain; thou hast scattered thine enemies with thy strong arm. Psalms 89:5-10.*

The Psalmist is asking questions of the congregation of the saints, the celestial host of heaven in this passage as confirmed by the "sons of the mighty" and "Lord God of hosts". He asks, "who in heaven can be compared unto the Lord?". One such being in heaven dared to compare himself, Lucifer. The Psalmist then declares the name of the one that dared, *Rahab,* who is "*...leviathan the piercing serpent, even leviathan that crooked serpent; and he shall slay the dragon that is in the sea*" Isaiah 27:1. Rahab, the dragon of the sea....

CHAPTER 4

RAHAB

The Psalmist just named the rebelling Lucifer Rahab, "the dragon, that old serpent, which is the Devil, and Satan" Revelation 20. One must ask at this point if Lucifer or Rahab is the name of Satan? Or was his name changed after he sinned to Rahab? Lucifer means light bearer, and the anointed cherub certainly displayed the Glory of God. *"...thou hast corrupted thy wisdom **by reason of thy brightness**:" Ezekiel 28:17*. He can also masquerade as an angel of light, *"And no marvel; for **Satan himself is transformed into an angel of light**" 2 Corinthians 11:14*. Lucifer was called "son of the morning," referring to the morning star of creation during that epoch. Rahab, in the context of leviathan, the dragon, means the proud one, fierceness, and arrogance.

*"How art thou fallen from heaven, O Lucifer, **son of the morning**! how art thou cut down to the*

ground, which didst weaken the nations!"
Isaiah 14:12

Could it be that Lucifer warred with God and became Rahab, much like Jacob wrestled with God and had his name changed to Israel? After wrestling with the Lord all night, Jacob finally surrendered, becoming victorious through the Lord. But Lucifer did not yield and, therefore, suffered the consequences. Jacob, a shepherd, became a prince, while Lucifer, created an eternal prince, would die like a man. *"And he said, Thy **name** shall be called no more **Jacob, but Israel**: for as a **prince** hast **thou power with God and with men**, and hast **prevailed"** Genesis 32:28.*

Continuing with Psalms 89, we will take a closer look at Rahab. In verse nine, the Psalmist mentions that God "rulest the raging of the sea.". This raging of the sea is a reference to the wicked. The sea is a dangerous place, a place that man cannot survive, a place wherein *"dead things are formed from under the waters"* Job 26:5. *"But the **wicked** are like the **troubled sea**, when it **cannot rest**, whose waters cast up **mire and dirt"** Isaiah 57:20.* *"**Raging waves of the sea**, foaming out their own shame; **wandering stars**, to whom is reserved the blackness of darkness for ever"* Jude 1:3. The Psalmist confirms that heaven and earth belong to God alone.

*"Thou rulest the **raging of the sea**: when the waves thereof arise, thou stillest them. Thou **hast broken Rahab in pieces**, as one that is **slain**; thou hast **scattered thine enemies** with thy **strong arm**. The **heavens are thine, the earth also is thine**: as for the world and the fulness thereof, thou hast founded them."*
Psalms 89:9-11

The emphasis now turns to Jesus. Mount Hermon has three summits, each within about ¼ mile of each other. Perhaps Tabor is the summit where the transfiguration of Jesus took place. *"And was **transfigured** before them: and his face did shine as the sun, and his raiment was white as the light"* Matthew 17:2. Tabor and Hermon rejoiced in the name of Jesus (Psalm 89:12) as he defeated death. Those that obtain salvation during the war for the Kingdom will make a joyful sound. *"O come, let us sing unto the LORD: let us make a **joyful noise** to the rock of our **salvation**"* Psalms 95:1.

*"The north and the south thou hast created them: **Tabor and Hermon** shall rejoice in thy name. Thou hast **a mighty arm**: strong is thy hand, and **high is thy right hand**. Justice and judgment are the habitation of thy throne: mercy and truth shall go before thy face. Blessed is the people that know*

the joyful sound: they shall walk, O LORD, in the light of thy countenance. In thy name shall they rejoice all the day: and in thy righteousness shall they be exalted. For thou art the glory of their strength: and in thy favour our horn shall be exalted. For the LORD is our defence; and the Holy One of Israel is our king."
Psalms 89:12-18

Turning now to Psalms 18, David is giving thanks unto the Lord for delivering him from the hand of all his enemies, and from the hand of King Saul just as God promised in Psalm 89:22-23.

*"I will love thee, O LORD, my strength. The LORD is my rock, and my fortress, and my deliverer; my God, my strength, in whom **I will trust**; my buckler, and the horn of my salvation, and my high tower. I will call upon the LORD, who is worthy to be praised: so shall **I be saved from mine enemies.** The sorrows of death compassed me, and the floods of ungodly men made me afraid. The sorrows of hell compassed me about: the snares of death prevented me. In my distress I **called upon the LORD,** and cried unto my God: he heard my voice out of his temple, and my cry came before him, even into his ears."*
Psalms 18:1-6

After verse six, David's tone changes dramatically. He speaks of the Lord's judgment in a very strong language that suggests he is not speaking of himself but rather looking into the past to an ancient judgment that took place in the cosmos, showing the mighty arm of God.

> *"Then the **Earth shook and trembled**; the foundations also of the hills moved and were shaken, because he was wroth. There went up a **smoke out of his nostrils, and fire out of his mouth devoured**: coals were kindled by it. He **bowed the heavens** also, and came down: and **darkness was under his feet**."*
> *Psalms 18:7-9*

The earth shook and trembled in fear because it saw what was coming: the wrath of God and destructive forces. "A *fire goeth before him, and burneth up his enemies* round about. His *lightnings enlightened the world*: the *Earth saw, and trembled. The hills melted like wax* at the *presence of the LORD, at the presence of the Lord of the whole Earth"* Psalm 97:3-5. The Lord bowed or bent/crushed the heavens, extinguishing the light of the stars as **darkness was under his feet** and "upon the face of the deep." It is interesting to note the characteristics of smoke from the Lord's nostrils and fire from his mouth were given to leviathan, the dragon of the sea. "*Out of* *his mouth go burning lamps, and sparks of fire leap out. Out of his nostrils goeth smoke, as out of a seething pot or caldron. His breath kindleth coals, and a flame goeth out of his mouth"* Job 41:19-21. Continuing in Psalms 18:

"And he rode upon a cherub and did fly: yea, he did fly upon the wings of the wind."
Psalms 18:10

The Lord of Host riding a single cherub reveals tremendous detail in this judgment scene. It was His choice of transport for the battle at hand since His judgment was towards Lucifer (also a cherub) and the fallen ones. At the end of the Tribulation, the Lord chooses to ride a celestial white horse into battle, an animal that pertains to men and battle, a stark difference. *"And I saw heaven opened, and behold a white horse; and he that sat upon him was called Faithful and True, and in righteousness he doth judge and make war"* Revelation 19:11.

"He made darkness his secret place; his pavilion round about him were dark waters and thick clouds of the skies. At the brightness that was before him his thick clouds passed, hail stones and coals of fire. The LORD also thundered in the heavens, and the Highest gave his voice; hail stones and coals of fire. Yea, he sent out his arrows, and scattered them; and he shot out

*lightnings, and **discomfited them**. Then the chan-nels of waters were seen, and the **foundations of the world were discovered** at **thy rebuke**, O LORD, at the **blast of the breath of thy nostrils**." Psalms 18:11-15*

The Lord sent out arrows, which may be the same as lightning, and scattered His enemies. This scattering is the same as *"Thou hast **broken Rahab in pieces, as one that is slain**; thou hast **scattered thine enemies** with thy strong arm" Psalms 89:10.* Lucifer was wounded as one that is slain, perhaps when he lost his celestial body. *"Awake, awake, put on strength, O arm of the LORD; awake, as in the **ancient days**, in the **generations of old**. Art thou not it that hath **cut Rahab**, and **wounded the dragon**?" Isaiah 51:9.* After Lucifer lost his celestial body and the Lord formed him into the crooked serpent (Job 26:13), he was placed in the sea, his natural abode, until his final judgment.

*"There go the **ships**: there is <u>**that**</u> leviathan, whom thou **hast made to play therein**" Psalms 104:26.*

The Antichrist, as one of the heads (kings, kingdoms) of Leviathan, will come out of the sea during the Tribulation to meet his doom, *"And I stood upon the sand of the sea, and saw a **beast** rise up **out of the sea**, having **seven heads*** *and ten horns, and upon his horns ten crowns, and upon his heads the name of blasphemy"* Revelation 13:1. The Antichrist is a composite of the previous seven heads. It is the eighth, the biblical number for new beginnings, the beginning of the Tribulation period. *"And the beast that was, and is not, even* **he is the eighth, and is of the seven,** *and goeth into perdition"* Revelation 17:10. *"In that day the LORD with his sore and great and strong sword shall punish* **leviathan the piercing serpent, even leviathan that crooked serpent;** *and he shall* **slay the dragon that is in the sea"** Isaiah 27:1. "In that day" refers to the Day of the Lord commencing at the end of the Tribulation when he will "slay the dragon." Now we shall turn to Psalms 74:

> *"O God, why hast thou* **cast us off for ever?** *why doth thine anger smoke against the sheep of thy pasture? Remember thy* **congregation,** *which thou hast* **purchased of old;** *the* **rod of thine inheritance,** *which* **thou hast redeemed;** *this* **mount Zion,** *wherein* **thou hast dwelt.** *Lift up thy feet unto the perpetual desolations; even all that the* **enemy hath done wickedly in the sanctuary.** *Thine enemies roar in the midst of thy congregations; they set up their* **ensigns** *for signs. A man was famous according as he had lifted up axes upon the thick trees. But now they break down the carved work thereof at once with axes and hammers.*

*They have **cast fire into thy sanctuary**, they have defiled by **casting down** the dwelling place of **thy name to the ground**. They said in their hearts, Let us destroy them together: they have burned up all the synagogues of God in the land. We see not our signs: there is no more any prophet: neither is there among us any that knoweth how long. O God, how long shall the **adversary reproach**? shall the **enemy blaspheme** thy name for ever? Why withdrawest thou thy hand, even **thy right hand**? pluck it out of thy bosom. For **God is my King of old, working salvation** in the midst of the Earth. Thou didst **divide the sea** by thy **strength**: thou **brakest the heads of the dragons** in the waters. Thou **brakest the heads of Leviathan in pieces**, and gavest him **to be meat** to the **people inhabiting the wilderness**. Thou didst cleave the **fountain and the flood**: thou driedst up mighty rivers. The **day** is thine, the **night** also is thine: thou hast **prepared the light and the sun**. Thou hast set all the borders of the Earth: thou hast **made summer and winter. Remember this,** that the **enemy hath reproached**, O LORD, and that the **foolish people have blasphemed** thy name. O deliver not the soul of thy turtledove unto the multitude of the wicked: forget not the congregation of thy poor for ever. Have respect **unto the***

*covenant: for the dark places of the Earth are full
of the habitations of cruelty."*
Psalms 74:1-20

In Psalms 74, the Psalmist is speaking out against the
adversary (the devil, 1 Peter 5:8) and his fallen concerning
their destructive hold over man from the time when God
took his "congregation" out of Egypt during the Exodus
until the devastation of the first temple (Solomon's temple)
by the Babylonians. Most of God's people had chosen to
turn to idols, "ensigns for signs," rather than worship the
one true God. Just as Lucifer was cast out of the Holy
Mountain, he worked hard to cast down the dwelling
place of God's name. The Psalmist is looking back in
remembrance of God's power, as man had become the
"rod of thine inheritance" whom "thou hast redeemed"
from death by His Son from "Mount Zion," God's eternal throne. Seeing the wickedness done in the sanctuary,
he asks God, "How long shall the adversary reproach?"
and why have you withdrawn "thy right hand" that is
Jesus, the destroyer of the enemy? He remembers, "God is
my King of old" now "working salvation" amongst man.
The Psalmist looks back at the dividing of the sea during
the Exodus when God parted the Red Sea, allowing the
Israelites to escape Pharoh and the pursuing Egyptians.

The Psalmist remembers the flood of Noah when

God cleaved "the fountain and the flood" and declared that the day and night, made for man, belongs to Him. He remembers how God, after the destruction of the planet, "prepared the light and the sun" and "made summer and winter" for man. He calls to remembrance the "enemy hath reproached" and captured the "foolish people" in his snare to blaspheme the name of the Lord. He pleads for deliverance from the "multitude of the wicked" and asks that God "have respect unto the covenant," (the covenant He had with **King David** Psalm 89:28, 34.)

Each of the heads of Rahab is referenced as a dragon, *"thou brakest the **heads of the dragons** in the **waters**. Thou brakest the **heads of leviathan** in pieces."* Pharaoh of the Exodus was the first head of Rahab to be broken. Pharaoh is named directly as the "dragon" in a prophecy against the remnant of the kingdom of Egypt for their betrayal against Israel, a yet future event since the tower of Syene located next to the Aswan dam did not exist at that time. The destruction of the Aswan Dam will fulfill this prophecy.

> *"Speak, and say, Thus saith the Lord GOD; Behold, I am against thee, Pharaoh **king of Egypt**, the **great dragon** that lieth in the midst of **his** rivers, which **hath said, My river is mine own, and I have made it for myself**."*
> *Ezekiel 29:3*

*"And all the inhabitants of Egypt shall know that I am the LORD, because they have been a **staff of reed to the house of Israel**. When they took hold of thee by thy hand, **thou didst break, and rend all their shoulder**: and when **they leaned upon thee**, thou brakest, and madest all their loins to be at a stand."*
Ezekiel 29:6-7

*"And the land of Egypt shall be desolate and waste; and they shall know that I am the LORD: because he hath said, The river is mine, and I have made it. Behold, therefore I am against thee, and against thy **rivers**, and I will make the land of Egypt **utterly waste and desolate**, from the tower of **Syene** even unto the **border of Ethiopia**."*
Ezekiel 29:9-10

After the Exodus while the Israelites inhabited the wilderness, the Lord sent serpents to bite the rebelling Israelites, and the only way they could be saved was to look upon a brass serpent raised on a pole, perhaps representing the "meat" given to them. (Psalms 74:14) Meat can either be physical or spiritual food. In this case, it was spiritual, symbolizing the coming crucifixion of Jesus when he defeated death, introduced into creation by the serpent.

*"And **the LORD sent fiery serpents** among the*

*people, and **they bit the people**; and much people of Israel died. Therefore the people came to Moses, and said, We have sinned, for we have **spoken against the LORD**, and against thee; pray unto the LORD, that he take away the serpents from us. And Moses prayed for the people. And the LORD said unto Moses, **Make thee a fiery serpent, and set it upon a pole**: and it shall come to pass, that every one that is bitten, when he looketh upon it, shall live. And Moses made a serpent of brass, and put it upon a pole, and it came to pass, that if a serpent had bitten any man, **when he beheld** the serpent of brass, **he lived**."*
Numbers 21:6-9

At the end of Job 40, God spoke to Job about the elephant, a beast of the land that He created with man, and stated, *"He is the **chief of the ways of God**..." Job 40:19.* Even though the elephant is not a predator, the other animals do not fear him unless he becomes wroth with them. He is the only animal that draws water into his nose and squirts it into his mouth to drink. He is confident of his strength and safety.

*"Behold now behemoth, **which I made with thee**; he **eateth grass** as an ox."*
Job 40:15

*"Surely the mountains bring him forth food, where **all the beasts of the field play.**"*
Job 40:20

*"Behold, he **drinketh up a river,** and hasteth not: **he trusteth** that he can **draw up Jordan** into his **mouth.** He taketh it with his eyes: his nose **pierceth through snares.**"*
Job 40:22-23

God then speaks in contrast about another beast. Leviathan, meaning twisted or coiled. Job 41 devotes the entire chapter to this creature of the sea, a creature in opposition to the ways of God. Leviathan is used exactly five times in the Bible. Remember, the number five means death 20% of the time, and here, leviathan ultimately has an appointment with death. All five biblical entries for leviathan are singular, for there is only one: Rahab, the dragon of the sea.

*"**Canst thou draw out leviathan** with an hook? or his tongue with a cord which thou lettest down? **Canst thou put an hook into his nose?** or bore his jaw through with a thorn? Will he **make many supplications** unto thee? will he **speak soft words** unto thee?"*
Job 41:1-3

The Lord begins by asking Job if he can draw Leviathan out of the sea to show how feeble man is against him, just as Job could do nothing when Satan was loosed against him and destroyed all his animals and family except his wife.

> *"Will he **make a covenant** with thee? wilt thou take him for a servant for ever?"*
> *Verse 4.*

Lucifer did make a covenant with God as a servant, but God made the covenant void. *"Thou hast made **void the covenant of thy servant**: thou hast profaned his crown by casting it to the ground"* Psalm 89:39.

> *"Wilt thou **play with him** as with a bird? or **wilt thou bind him** for thy maidens?"*
> *Job 41:5*

Leviathan was made to "play" in the sea. *"There go the ships: there is that leviathan, whom thou hast **made to play therein**."* Psalms 104:26

> *"Shall the companions make a banquet of him? shall they part him among the merchants? Canst thou fill his skin with barbed irons? or his head with fish spears? Lay thine hand upon him, **remember the battle**, do no more."*
> *Job 41:6-8*

God tells Job to lay his hand on him and remember the battle, the great galactic battle.

> *"Behold, the hope of him is in vain: shall not one be cast down even at the sight of him?* **None is so fierce that dare stir him up: who then is able to stand before me? Who hath prevented me, that I should repay him?** *whatsoever is* **under the whole heaven** *is mine."*
> *Job 41:9-11*

No other created being dares to rouse the dragon. God then establishes that God alone is the most powerful in all creation. None can prevent the Lord from taking vengeance on the dragon. All of creation belongs to him. *"Dearly beloved, avenge not yourselves, but rather give place unto wrath: for it is written,* **Vengeance is mine; I will repay,** *saith the Lord." Romans 12:19*

> *"I will not conceal his parts, nor his power, nor his comely proportion. Who can discover the face of his garment? or who can come to him with his double bridle? Who can open the doors of his face? his teeth are terrible round about.* **His scales are his pride,** *shut up together as with a close seal. One is so near to another, that no air can come between them. They are joined one to another, they stick together, that they cannot be sundered.*

*By his **neesings** a **light doth shine**, and his eyes are like the **eyelids of the morning**. Out of his mouth go **burning lamps, and sparks of fire leap out**. Out of his **nostrils goeth smoke**, as out of a seething pot or caldron. 21 **His breath kindleth coals, and a flame goeth out of his mouth.**"*
Job 41:12-21

"Neesings" is used just once in the Bible with most interpretations referring to sneezing; however, remember that quartz stones are known to produce an electrical current when squeezed. When a person sneezes, their core tightens up like a squeeze. Could it be that by these neesings, the leviathan can produce fire and smoke, just as a dragon is depicted?

*"In his neck remaineth strength, and sorrow is turned into joy before him. The flakes of his flesh are joined together: they are firm in themselves; they cannot be moved. His **heart** is as **firm as a stone**; yea, as hard as a piece of the **nether millstone**. When he raiseth up himself, the **mighty are afraid**: by reason of breakings they purify themselves. The sword of him that layeth at him cannot hold: the spear, the dart, nor the habergeon. He esteemeth iron as straw, and brass as rotten wood. The arrow cannot make him flee: slingstones are*

turned with him into stubble. Darts are counted
as stubble: he laugheth at the shaking of a spear.
Sharp stones are under him: he spreadeth sharp
pointed things upon the mire."
Job 41:22-30

His heart is hardened like the stones of the pit. In battle,
no earthly weapon can harm him.

He maketh the deep to boil like a pot: he maketh
the sea like a pot of ointment. He maketh a path
to shine after him; one would think the deep to
be hoary. **Upon Earth there is not his like, who is**
made without fear. *He beholdeth* **all high things**:
he is a **king over all the children** *of pride.*
Job 41:31-34

He is the fearless prince of this world and king of pride, and
resides within Rahab, the dragon of the sea. *"Now is the*
judgment of this world: now shall the **prince of this world**
*be cast out." John 12:31 "****Pride** *goeth before* **destruction,**
and an **haughty spirit** *before a* **fall."** *Proverbs 16:18*

CHAPTER 5

THE HARLOT

Turning our attention to Psalm 87, the Psalmist writes about Zion/Jerusalem, the future abode of God, where he has chosen to complete his work concerning redemption. Glorious things are spoken of there. This is the first of three mentions of Rahab referring to the dragon.

> *"His foundation is in the holy mountains. The LORD loveth the gates of Zion more than all the dwellings of Jacob. Glorious things are spoken of thee, O city of God. Selah. I will make mention of **Rahab** and **Babylon** to them that know me: behold **Philistia**, and **Tyre**, with **Ethiopia**; this man was born there."*
> *Psalm 87:1-4*

Looking deeper at this Psalm, the Lord speaks of specific names associated with Rahab; four are place names. We have already established that Rahab is the dragon, the fallen Lucifer. Babylon is the city in which the tribes were held during their second captivity, and the city that will rise once again during the Tribulation to be known for its apostate religion, whoredom, and prolific commerce. Philistia, the early arch enemy of Israel known as the Philistines, and Tyre, the city of markets and trade that knew not God. Ethiopia is also an enemy of Israel and a distant country expressing the long arm of the Lord whether to pronounce judgment or salvation.

There is a curious lumping together when the Lord mentions Rahab and Babylon "to them that know me." They are clearly connected in the scriptures, as we shall see shortly. Rahab of Jericho, mentioned seven times, was known as a "harlot" (Joshua 2:1), and Rahab in the Hebrew definition for these seven entries means "wide", perhaps a crass reference to her occupation. However, she became faithful to the God of Israel by hiding two Israelite spies when the king of Jericho sent men to capture the spies, and she was saved by her faith and repentance. Rahab, the dragon in Hebrew, indicates "breadth" and we are quickly reminded of the verses *"Enter ye in at the strait gate: for **wide** is the gate, and **broad** is the way, that leadeth to destruction, and many there be which go in thereat:"* Matthew 7:13. For *"The thief cometh not, but for to **steal**, and to **kill**, and to **destroy**"* John 10:10. The breadth of destruction from the Devil is broad and wide, and Hell was *"...prepared for the devil and his* angels:" *Matthew 25:41*. Babylon of the Tribulation, a city of confusion, will be known as a harlot. *"And upon her forehead was a name written, MYSTERY, BABYLON THE GREAT, THE MOTHER OF HARLOTS AND ABOMINATIONS OF THE EARTH" Revelation 17:5*.

Chapters 13 and 14 of Isaiah speak of the judgment against Babylon, past and future. We will look at chapter 14 to see the connection between Rahab and Babylon. The King of the ancient city of Babylon was King Nebuchadnezzar. Isaiah takes up a proverb against the king of Babylon starting in verse four. The proverb uses Nebuchadnezzar as the ancient king, or Rahab as the spiritual king for the coming Babylon of the Tribulation.

"That thou shalt take up this proverb against the king of Babylon, and say, How hath the *oppressor* ceased! the golden city ceased! The LORD hath *broken the staff of the wicked*, and the *sceptre of the rulers*. He who *smote the people in wrath* with a *continual stroke*, he that *ruled the nations in anger*, is *persecuted*, and none hindereth. The *whole earth is at rest*, and is quiet: they break forth into singing. Yea, the fir trees rejoice at thee, and the cedars of Lebanon, saying, Since thou art laid down, *no feller is come up against us. Hell* from beneath is *moved for thee to meet thee at thy coming*: it stirreth up the dead for thee, even

all the chief ones of the earth; it hath raised up from their thrones *all the kings of the nations.* All they shall speak and say unto thee, Art thou *also become weak* as we? art thou *become like unto us?* Thy *pomp* is brought down to the grave, and the noise of *thy viols*: the worm is spread under thee, and the worms cover thee. How art thou fallen from heaven, O *Lucifer*, son of the morning! how art thou cut down to the ground, which didst weaken the nations!"
Isaiah 14:4-12

The **oppressor** was called out in Isaiah 14 above. Jesus will *"... judge the poor of the people, he shall save the children of the needy, and shall break in pieces the oppressor"* *Psalms 72:4*, just as he broke the heads of leviathan-Rahab into pieces. At the end of the Tribulation, Jesus will break the "staff of the wicked" (Antichrist) and the "sceptre of the rulers" (10 Kings of Tribulation, Revelation 17:12). Satan has smitten the people in "continual stroke" since the time of Adam, and has "ruled the nations in anger" as the "god of this world" 2 Corinthians 4:4. The "whole earth is at rest" with the enemies defeated. Satan's pomp, or show of grandeur and the "noise of thy viols" (*"the workmanship of thy tabrets and of thy pipes" Ezekiel 28:13*), is put to rest. The Devil is cast into Hell and those there who served him throughout the ages shall ask, "Have you 'also become weak as we?'" The spiritual King of Babylon is named "Lucifer, son of the morning," – *Rahab*.

> *"And I saw an angel come down from heaven, having the key of the **bottomless pit** and a **great chain in his hand**. And he **laid hold on the dragon, that old serpent**, which is the **Devil, and Satan,** and bound him a thousand years, And **cast him into the bottomless pit**, and shut him up, and set a seal upon him, that he should deceive the nations no more, till the thousand years should be fulfilled: and after that he must be loosed a little season."*
> *Revelation 20:1-3*

Moving down in Isaiah 14, we read:

> *"The LORD of hosts hath sworn, saying, Surely as I have thought, so **shall it come to pass;** and as I have purposed, so shall it stand: That I will **break the Assyrian in my land,** and **upon my mountains tread him under foot:** then shall his yoke depart from off them, and his burden depart from off their shoulders. This is the purpose that is purposed upon the **whole earth:** and this is the hand that is stretched out upon **all the nations.** For the LORD of hosts hath purposed, and who shall disannul it? and his hand is stretched out,*

and who shall turn it back? In the year that king
Ahaz died was this burden."
Isaiah 14:24-28

The Lord announces judgment on the Assyrians by an
angel of the Lord, *"And it came to pass that night, that*
the angel of the LORD went out, and smote in the camp
of the Assyrians an hundred fourscore and five thousand:
and when they arose early in the morning, behold, they
*were **all dead corpses"** 2 Kings 19:35.* This judgment also
looks to the future "Assyrian," the Antichrist who the
Lord will break in his land upon his mountains and tread
him underfoot (Genesis 3:15) removing the burdensome
yoke from the people of the whole earth and all nations.
Now the Lord turns to Palestina to declare judgment. This
is the connection to Philistia from Psalm 87:4.

*"Rejoice not thou, **whole Palestina,** because the*
rod of him that smote thee is broken: for out
*of the **serpent's root** shall come forth a **cocka-***
trice,** and his fruit shall be a **fiery flying serpent.
And the firstborn of the poor shall feed, and the
needy shall lie down in safety: and I will kill thy
root with famine, and he shall slay thy remnant.
*Howl, O gate; cry, **O city; thou, whole Palestina,***
***art dissolved:** for there shall come from the north*
a smoke, and none shall be alone in his appointed

times. What shall one then answer the messen-
*gers of the nation? That the LORD hath **founded***
***Zion** (**Psalm 87**), and the poor of his people shall*
trust in it."
Isaiah 14:29-31

The Assyrians had previously conquered Palestina, so
the Lord instructs the Philistines not to rejoice in the
Assyrians' destruction in Isaiah 14:29 mentioned above,
for they would meet their own fate when King Hezekiah
of Judah would "*...**smote the Philistines**, even unto Gaza,*
and the borders thereof, from the tower of the watchmen
to the fenced city" *2 Kings 18:8*. Again, looking to the
future, this also declares a prophecy "out of the serpent's
root shall come forth a cockatrice" Isaiah 14:29, that is to
say, from Satan will come the Antichrist. The Antichrist
will establish his headquarters in Jerusalem, but the whole
of Palestina shall not escape, and the **Ethiopians,** who at
times were a terror to Israel and were previously slain by
the sword of the Lord (Zephaniah 2:12), shall be under his
grasp, his beck and call.

"He shall enter also into the glorious land, and
***many countries shall be overthrown:** but these*
shall escape out of his hand, even Edom, and
Moab, and the chief of the children of Ammon.
*He shall **stretch forth his hand also upon the***

> *countries: and the **land of Egypt shall not escape.***
> *But he shall have power over the treasures of gold*
> *and of silver, and over all the precious things of*
> *Egypt: and the Libyans and the **Ethiopians shall***
> ***be at his steps.***"
> *Daniel 11:41-45.*

Looking back at Psalm 87, we have made a connection to
Rahab from three of the four named in verse 4. Only Tyre
remains, but that is easy to identify since Lucifer is named
the King of Tyre in Ezekiel 28.

> "*Moreover the word of the LORD came unto me,*
> *saying, Son of man, take up a lamentation upon*
> *the **king of Tyrus**, and say unto him, Thus saith*
> *the Lord GOD; Thou sealest up the sum, full of*
> *wisdom, and perfect in beauty.*"
> *Ezekiel 28:11-12*

> "*Take an harp, go about the city, thou **harlot** that*
> *hast been forgotten; make sweet melody, sing*
> *many songs, that thou mayest be remembered.*
> *And it shall come to pass after the end of seventy*
> *years, that the LORD will visit **Tyre**, and she*
> *shall turn to her hire, and shall **commit fornica-***
> ***tion with all the kingdoms of the world** upon the*
> *face of the earth.*"
> *Isaiah 23:16-17*

The city of Tyre was the center of the commercial system, a worldly system that replaced God with fame, power, merchandise and wealth for many people. This commercial system will only grow more significant into the Tribulation as the city of Babylon takes the lead. None will be able to buy or sell without the mark. *"And he causeth all, both small and great, rich and poor, free and bond, to receive a* **mark** *in their right hand, or in their foreheads: And that* **no man might buy or sell**, *save he that had the mark, or the name of the beast, or the number of his name."* *Revelation 13:16-17*

Now looking at the Psalm as a whole, it seems to be a division between those born into the Devil's realm and those born of God through Jesus, his Savior from Zion. The Lord "shall count" and "writeth up the people" Psalm 87:6 into the Book of Life. All the springs of life are in Zion. The war for the Kingdom.

> **"His foundation is in the holy mountains.** *The* LORD **loveth the gates of Zion** *more than all the dwellings of Jacob. Glorious things are spoken of thee, O city of God. Selah. I will make mention of* **Rahab** *and* **Babylon** *to them that know me: behold* **Philistia**, *and* **Tyre**, *with* **Ethiopia**; *this* **man was born there.** *And of* **Zion** *it* **shall be said**, *This and that man was* **born in her:** *and the*

highest himself shall establish her. The LORD
shall count, when he writeth up the people, that
this man was born there. Selah. As well the sing-
ers as the players on instruments shall be there:
all my springs are in thee."
Psalm 87

The author admits that some of the following is speculation. Often, Scripture can have a dual meaning. The Hebrew definition for each of these names from Psalm 87:4 may also possibly describe the ancient fifth planet once located between Mars and Jupiter. This area is now known as the asteroid belt. However, it is certain the asteroid belt once was a planet, for God does not fail at creation, as some scientists speculate. It is assumed the asteroid fields are the remains of a failed attempt of a planet whose gravitational field was too weak to keep it intact. Some biblical scholars have named this planet Rahab, perhaps because it is now in "pieces." The author is undecided about the name placement, but is convinced it once was a planet and will use the name "fifth planet" for easy identification going forward. We will look into the list below in more detail.

Rahab = wide/breadth

Babylon = confusion (by mixing)

Philistia = land of sojourners

Tyre = a rock

Ethiopia = Black

The fifth planet was brooding with the Devil (Rahab) and the fallen ones. Its explosion caused an immense breadth of destruction within the Solar System. It was the harlot of the solar system, an abomination unto the Lord just as the future Babylon will be the harlot of Earth. The former was previously destroyed, while the latter is yet to be. Like Babylon, the fifth planet had become *"...the habitation of devils, and the hold of every foul spirit,"* Revelation 18:2. The planet was not intended to be a natural habitat for the fallen ones. It was the land of sojourners, as Philistia describes in its' Hebrew definition. It was the distant, rocky planet as noted by Tyre, and black like Ethiopia, void of God's light. It is not clear in what way the fifth planet had become a harlot, but it was perhaps a stronghold of Lucifer inundated with his traffick, merchandise, holding of prisoners, and violence. Nevertheless, nothing can be hidden from God, and their dirty deeds would not go undiscovered.

> *"Thou hast **broken down** all his **hedges**; thou hast brought his **strong holds** to **ruin**."*
> *Psalms 89:40*

The fifth planet was in direct opposition to the will of God. Unlike what we have seen with Noah's flood and Sodom and Gomorrah, the level of wickedness and vileness was so great, that God chose to destroy the wicked planet completely into pieces, making a "full end" of it. This explosion would undoubtedly mar the solar system with destruction, including planet Earth, the home of Lucifer's throne, leaving it "void and without form" Genesis 1:2. Despite that, God chose not to make a "full end" of Earth.

> *"I beheld the earth, and, lo, it was without form, and void; and the heavens, and they had no light. I beheld the mountains, and, lo, they trembled, and all the hills moved lightly. I beheld, and, lo, there was no man, and all the birds of the heavens were fled. I beheld, and, lo, the fruitful place was a wilderness, and all the cities thereof were broken down at the presence of the LORD, and by his fierce anger. For thus hath the LORD said, **The whole land shall be desolate; yet will I not make a full end.**"*
> *Jeremiah 4:23-27*

CHAPTER 6

DESTRUCTION

It is essential to understand that God chose to use the heavens to articulate His plan and story before the written Word, which did not come along until at least the time of Moses, some 2,000 years after Adam. The night sky was much more vibrant and eventful than today, and some planets had different orbits. Can you imagine the majesty of the heavens without any air pollution or artificial light? Perhaps even the atmosphere was different up until the time of Noah's flood. The messages the heavens articulated were so crucial that the enemy quickly corrupted them to become a form of false worship among men. Even the Israelites fell prey to this trap, worshiping the stars and planets as gods. Today, some cultures still worship the heavens, the original messages corrupted by the Devil into modern-day astrology, and what was this "image which fell down from Jupiter"?

"The heavens declare the glory of God; and the firmament sheweth his handywork. Day unto day uttereth speech, and night unto night sheweth knowledge. There is no speech nor language, where their voice is not heard. Their line is gone out through all the earth, and their words to the end of the world."
Psalms 19:1-4

"And lest thou lift up thine eyes unto heaven, and when thou seest the sun, and the moon, and the stars, even all the host of heaven, shouldest be driven to worship them, and serve them, which the LORD thy God hath divided unto all nations under the whole heaven."
Deuteronomy 4:19

"And he put down the idolatrous priests, whom the kings of Judah had ordained to burn incense in the high places in the cities of Judah, and in the places round about Jerusalem; them also that burned incense unto Baal, to the sun, and to the moon, and to the planets, and to all the host of heaven."
2 Kings 23:5

"And when the people saw what Paul had done, they lifted up their voices, saying in the speech of Lycaonia, The gods are come down to us in

the likeness of men. 12 And they called Barnabas,
***Jupiter;** and Paul, **Mercurius,** because he was the*
*chief speaker. 13 Then the **priest of Jupiter,** which*
was before their city, brought oxen and garlands
unto the gates, and would have done sacrifice
with the people."
Acts 14:12-13

"And when the townclerk had appeased the people,
he said, Ye men of Ephesus, what man is there that
knoweth not how that the city of the Ephesians is
a worshipper of the great goddess Diana, and of
the image which fell down from Jupiter?"
Acts 19:35

We will now look deeper into the fifth planet. Lucifer had
10 precious stones embedded in his body. While gold is
technically a chemical element and a mineral, in this reference, the Bible calls it a precious stone (Ezekiel 28:13). First,
we must establish the Biblical meanings for the numbers
10 and 5. The number 10 refers to the whole unit, the
full measure of something. Ten encompasses all digits, one
through zero. Examples include the Ten Commandments
and the ten plaques of Egypt. Abraham negotiated with
God not to destroy Sodom with the righteous people, and
10 was the final number of the whole unit. *"And he said,*
Oh let not the Lord be angry, and I will speak yet but

this once: Peradventure **ten shall be found there.** *And he said I will not destroy it* **for ten's sake"** *Genesis 18:32.* *"Because all those men which have seen my glory, and my miracles, which I did in Egypt and in the wilderness, and* **have tempted me** *now these* **ten times,** *and have not hearkened to my voice;"* Numbers 14:22. The ten kings of Revelation. The number five represents a divine appointment with God, whether it be an appointment with grace, death, judgment, etc. Five represents death 20% of the time in the Bible.

> *"And they slew the kings of Midian, beside the rest of them that were slain; namely, Evi, and Rekem, and Zur, and Hur, and Reba,* **five kings** *of Midian:"* Numbers 31:8.

> *"And he took his staff in his hand, and chose him* **five smooth stones** *out of the brook, and put them in a shepherd's bag which he had, even in a scrip; and his sling was in his hand: and he drew near to the Philistine"* 1 Samuel 17:40

> *"In that day shall* **five cities** *in the land of Egypt speak the language of Canaan, and swear to the LORD of hosts; one shall be called, The city of destruction."* Isaiah 19:18

Perhaps the 10 precious stones embedded into Lucifer also represented the 10 planets of creation as the "stones of fire." Just like he *"wast upon the **holy mountain** of God; thou hast walked up and down in the midst of the stones of fire" Ezekiel 28:14*, could he also walk up and down the solar system? Looking at the stones again, *"...every precious stone was thy covering, the sardius, topaz, and the **diamond**, the beryl, the **onyx**, and the jasper, the sapphire, the emerald, and the carbuncle, and gold:" Ezekiel 28:13.* Neither the diamond nor the onyx will be used again in the future as one of the 12 precious stones for the city of New Jerusalem. The diamond is the third stone and would represent the earth. Remember, the diamond was the only stone that is isotropic, one that will not produce light with a ray of light passing through as if God knew the earth given to Lucifer would end in darkness, void, and without form. The fifth stone, the onyx, is typically black like Ethiopia from the previous chapter, meaning black in Hebrew. Here, the fifth stone is associated with death, as that planet was destroyed. Lucifer can be seen as the fifth cherub: four cherubs carried the throne of God while Lucifer, the fifth, was the cherub that covereth. And then there are the fateful five "I will's" he uttered. Lucifer ultimately has been assigned to death. God said. *"... I will destroy thee, O covering cherub, **from the midst** of the **stones of fire**" Ezekiel 28:16.* The fifth planet would have been amid the 10 planets, and perhaps it was here during the galactic war in which Lucifer's perfect body was destroyed to become Rahab.

The planets would have been much **closer before God created the firmament and stretched** out the heaven. How much closer, we don't know. It is very possible God used the planet Mars to destroy the fifth planet. Mars' late orbit was much different than its modern orbit, which did not commence until possibly 701 B.C. with its last near-earth fly-by. The two moons of Mars had been highly detailed in description, including size, rotation, and revolutions, at least 150 years before their discovery in 1877 by Asaph Hall, who used a new telescope at the U.S. Naval Observatory. In 701 B.C., the second King of Rome, Numa Pompilius, added 5 days to the 360-day calendar. Was the calendar addition a result of the influence Mars had on Earth's orbit? It has been suggested that Mars was the cause of many upheavals here on Earth during the Old Testament era. Whether or not Mars was the cause of destruction, one thing is clear: Mars and earth, along with the fifth planet, converged in their orbits at the time of destruction. Mars is the most scarred planet in the solar system, and rightfully so, as it was not renewed like Earth.

There are no oceans, lakes, or rivers on Mars, and it has minimal atmosphere. The escape velocity of Mars is too weak to hold water, as is evident in the absence of oxygen and water vapor. Yet there is massive evidence of catastrophic flash flooding almost all within the eastern hemisphere of Mars, including various types of water channels and dry riverbeds up to 400 miles in length. Asteroids have been found to contain water molecules. Watery ice globes exist today in the solar system. According to NASA, at least six of Saturn's many moons are made up of mostly water and ice. Was the fifth planet a massive, watery, ice planet? Could it be the explosion of the fifth planet pushed an untold amount of water into space, hitting the eastern hemisphere of Mars while the majority made its way to Earth? That would explain the catastrophic flooding on Mars and *"...the earth standing out of the water and in the water"* 2 Peter 3:5, and *"... **darkness** was upon the face of the **deep**. And the Spirit of God moved upon the **face of the waters**"* Genesis 1:2. Those waters would have issued forth like from a womb. If you have ever seen a mammal or human birthed from the womb, you know how this looks. The walls of water and rain pouring down would have been unlike anything the earth had known. This is one reason God stretched the heaven, created the firmament, and placed the massive amounts of water below and above the firmament. There was no man on the earth when this happened.

> *"Or who **shut up the sea with doors**, when it **brake forth**, as if it had **issued out of the womb**? When I made the cloud the garment thereof, **and thick darkness** a swaddlingband for it, And*

*brake up for it **my decreed place**, and set bars and doors, And said, Hitherto shalt thou come, but no further: and here shall thy proud waves be stayed?"*
Job 38:8-11

"To <u>cause it</u> to **rain on the earth, where no man is**; on the **wilderness, wherein there is no man**;"
Job 38:26

*"And every plant of the field before it was in the earth, and every herb of the field before it **grew**: for the LORD God **had <u>not</u> caused** it to **rain upon the earth**, and there was not a man to till the ground. But there **went up a mist from the earth**, and **watered the whole face** of the ground."*
Genesis 2:5-6

Mars was also hit by enormous asteroid impacts. Asteroids are heavier than water and were estimated to travel around 25,000 mph, hitting Mars well before the water arrived if the water came from the fifth planet. It seems the fifth planet was approaching Mars on a lower plane from the rear when it exploded. There are thousands of impact craters on Mars, with roughly 93%, including the largest on one side of the globe towards its southern hemisphere. Mars has the largest confirmed impact crater known in the solar system, called the Utopia Planitia, at 2,100 miles in diameter. The next three largest are Hellas at 1,400 miles, Isidis at 1,200, and Argyre at 1,100—the next 20 largest range from 200 to 300 miles in diameter. Keep in mind the circumference of Mars is only around 13,000 miles. On its opposite side are very large volcanic regions caused by these asteroid impacts pushing into the core. The largest is Olympus Mons, which is 13.6 miles high or 2.5 times the elevation of Mount Everest and is tied for the tallest known mountain in the solar system. The edifice or cone of Olympus Mons is approximately 370 miles wide, while the entire mountain covers an area of 120,000 square miles. The second largest is Ascraeus Mons at an elevation of 11 miles and a cone 300 miles wide. Again, opposite of the crater impacts is a rift or crack in the Martian crust. This crack is some 2,500 miles long, or 19% of the circumference of Mars. It is 4.5 miles deep and up to 375 miles wide. The Grand Canyon, in comparison, is 500 miles long, 18 miles wide, and 1 mile deep. All of this is on a planet that has 10% of the mass of Earth.

Our moon is also heavily scarred. Most of the moon's craters reside on the far side. The three largest impact craters on the moon are Procellarum at 2,000 miles wide, Aitken Basin at 1,600 miles, and Imbrium at 711 miles in diameter. Mars is about twice the size of the moon. The moon has a rotational period of 27 days. The barrage of large asteroids was still immense even at this distance from the 5th planet, which is more evidence that the planets were closer then. We do not know what size craters these asteroids had at impact on Earth. All we know is after the impacts, "...*the earth was without form, and void*" *Genesis 1:2.* "*And God said, Let the waters under the heaven be gathered together unto one place, and let the dry land appear: and it was so*" *Genesis 1:9.* "*The sea is his, and he made it: and his hands formed the dry land*" *Psalms 95:5.* God had formed the dry land, likely removing these large impacts. Today, the largest impact craters on Earth are the Vredefort, between 160 and 190 miles in width, the Chicxulub crater at 113 miles, and Sudbury Basin at 80 miles. A mere drop in the bucket compared to Mars and the Moon. These newer, smaller impact carters may have been remnants of the fifth planet knocked out of orbit and could have been part of what caused the Ice Age around the time of Job's life on Earth. The waters were hidden with icebergs, and the face of the oceans were frozen. Again, the Ice Age was a sudden event, as shown by the womb/gendered scenario.

> "*Out of whose **womb** came the **ice**? and the hoary frost of heaven, who hath **gendered it**? The waters are hid as with a **stone**, and the face of the deep is frozen.*"
> *Job 38:29-30*

Looking back at the initial impact of asteroids from the fifth planet, the Earth saw these asteroids and a wall of water coming at her. This passage speaks of that time and commands the gods, the fallen ones, to worship the God of Heaven. The hills melted from these catastrophic collisions.

> *"The LORD reigneth; let the earth rejoice; let the multitude of isles be glad thereof.* **Clouds and darkness are round about him**: *righteousness and judgment are the habitation of his throne. A* **fire** *goeth before him,* **and burneth up his enemies** *round about. His lightnings enlightened the world:* **the earth saw, and trembled.** *The* **hills melted like wax** *at the presence of the LORD, at the presence of the Lord of the whole earth. The* **heavens declare his righteousness,** *and all the people see his glory. Confounded be all they that serve graven images, that boast themselves of idols:* **worship him, all ye gods.***"*
> *Psalms 97:1-7*

Lucifer had hardened himself against God and suffered the consequences. The Earth was shaken out of her place, hence the 23-degree axis tilt from zero. The mountains were thrown down. The Sun and stars went black, *"And God said,* **Let there be light**: *and there was light."* *Genesis 1:3.*

> *"He is wise in heart, and mighty in strength:* **who hath hardened himself against him, and hath**

prospered? Which removeth the mountains, and they know not: which overturneth them in his anger. Which shaketh the earth out of her place, and the pillars thereof tremble. Which commandeth the sun, and it riseth not; and sealeth up the stars. Which alone spreadeth out the heavens, and treadeth upon the waves of the sea. Which maketh Arcturus, Orion, and Pleiades, and the chambers of the south. Which doeth great things past finding out; yea, and wonders without number."
Job 9:4-10

Even Heaven trembled at the Lord's rebuke. The Lord did smite the proud Lucifer and formed Rahab.

"The pillars of heaven tremble and are astonished at his reproof. He divideth the sea with his power, and by his understanding he smiteth through the proud. By his spirit he hath garnished the heavens; his hand hath formed the crooked serpent. Lo, these are parts of his ways: but how little a portion is heard of him? but the thunder of his power who can understand?"
Job 26:11-14

One day, perhaps, we will know the full extent of what happened during that galactic war. Why were the fallen ones on the fifth planet in the first place? Were they mining a specific mineral for an energy source to create a weapon against God? As in all battles, weapons of various kinds are used against the other side. It is interesting to note Iridium is a good conductor of heat and electricity. Asteroids contain high levels of Iridium; however, Iridium is a rare earth element but found in very high concentrations, up to 100 times greater than usual, in a thin worldwide layer of clay within the earth between the Cretaceous and Paleogene periods, some 66 million years ago according to the scientific community. Coincidently, this is the period most often mentioned for the extinction of the dinosaurs within the scientific community. For the record, this author does not think the earth is anywhere near that old. We cannot determine the time from when Lucifer sinned until Genesis 1:2. "....He was a murderer *from the beginning* ..." John 8:44. Perhaps in terms of time created for man, the Earth is no more than 15,000 years old. God will once again use asteroids or equivalents to bring destruction and judgment upon the Earth.

"And the second angel sounded, and as it were a ***great mountain burning*** *with fire was cast into the sea: and the third part of the sea became blood."* *Revelation 8:8*

CHAPTER 7

LORD OF HOSTS

The Lord of Host, Jesus, is a warrior. Like all kingdoms, God's kingdom has an army and ranks within that army to protect against threats. There are ordinances, dominions, judges, and rules that all, even Satan must abide by.

> *"The LORD is a man of war: the LORD is his name."*
> *Exodus 15:3*

> *"Wherefore it is said in the book of the wars of the LORD, What he did in the Red sea, and in the brooks of Arnon,"*
> *Numbers 21:14*

> *"Is there any number of his armies? and upon whom doth not his light arise?"*
> *Job 25:3*

> *"Hast thou entered into the treasures of the*

snow? or hast thou seen the treasures of the hail,
Which I have reserved against the time of trouble,
*against the **day of battle and war?***"
Job 38:22-23

"*Who is this King of glory? The LORD strong*
*and mighty, **the LORD mighty in battle**. Lift up*
your heads, O ye gates; even lift them up, ye ever-
lasting doors; and the King of glory shall come in.
*Who is this King of glory? **The LORD of hosts**, he*
*is the **King of glory**. Selah.*"
Psalm 24

"*For we wrestle not against flesh and blood, but*
*against **principalities**, against **powers**, against the*
rulers of the darkness** of this world, against **spir-
***itual wickedness** in high places.*"
Ephesians 6:12

"*Knowest thou the **ordinances of heaven?** canst*
*thou set the **dominion** thereof in the earth?*"
Job 38:33

In this present day, the Lord will soon avenge all enemies of his kingdom, the innocent blood that has been spilled, the unrighteous judgments, and the Adversary beginning in Heaven. For even the gods, the fallen ones shall be judged and die like men.

    "*And they cried with a loud voice, saying, How long,*

*O Lord, holy and true, dost thou not **judge and avenge our blood** on them that dwell on the earth?"*
Revelation 6:10

*"O God, **how long shall the adversary reproach? shall the enemy blaspheme** thy name for ever?"*
Psalms 74:10

*"God standeth in the **congregation of the mighty;** he judgeth among the **gods.** How long will ye **judge unjustly,** and accept the persons of the wicked? Selah. Defend the poor and fatherless: do justice to the afflicted and needy. Deliver the poor and needy: rid them out of the hand of the wicked. They know not, neither will they understand; they walk on in darkness: **all the foundations of the earth are out of course.** I have said, **Ye are gods;** and all of you are **children of the most High.** But ye shall **die like men,** and **fall like one of the princes.** Arise, O God, judge the earth: for thou shalt inherit all nations."*
Psalms 82

*"Behold my servant, whom I uphold; mine elect, in whom my soul delighteth; I have put my spirit upon him: **he shall bring forth judgment to the Gentiles.**"*
Isaiah 42:1

*"The **LORD** shall go forth as a **mighty man,** he*

*shall stir up jealousy like a **man of war**: he shall cry, yea, roar; he shall prevail against **his enemies**. I have **long time holden my peace**; I have been still, and refrained myself: now will I cry like a travailing woman; I will **destroy** and **devour** at once."*
Isaiah 42:13-14

*"For my **sword shall be bathed in heaven**: behold, **it shall come down** upon Idumea, and upon the people of my curse, to judgment. The **sword of the LORD** is filled with blood..."*
Is 34:5-6

*"And the winepress was trodden without the city, and **blood came out of the winepress**, even unto the horse bridles, by the space of a thousand and six hundred furlongs."*
Revelation 14:20

*"And he was clothed with a **vesture dipped in blood**: and his name is called The Word of God."*
Revelation 19:13

When God created, the energy of His voice was turned into matter, similar to the famous Einstein equation E=MC2, the kinetic energy of an object is equal to the mass of the object times the speed of light squared. All matter can be considered a form of energy. God's voice is a form of energy, which creates or makes matter. As the One that created all matter, the properties of Physics obey His voice. From the Genesis account, each day it was stated, "*...and God said...*" then something was created or made "*...by the word of his power...*" God can also use His voice to destroy.

> *"Who being the brightness of his glory, and the express image of his person, and upholding all things by the **word of his power**, when he had by himself purged our sins, sat down on the right hand of the Majesty on high."*
> *Hebrews 1:3*

> *"He hath made the earth by his **power**, he hath established the world by his wisdom, and hath stretched out the heavens by his discretion."*
> *Jeremiah 10:12*

> *"Lo, these are parts of his ways: but how little a portion is heard of him? but the **thunder** of his **power** who can understand?"*
> *Job 26:14*

> *"Repent; or else I will come unto thee quickly, and will fight against them with the **sword of my mouth**."*
> *Revelation 2:16*

*"And **out of his mouth goeth a sharp sword,** that with it he should **smite the nations:** and he shall rule them with a rod of iron: and he treadeth the winepress of the fierceness and wrath of Almighty God."*
Revelation 19:15

The entire creation is in disarray and desires to be reconciled back to God, all that is in Heaven, and all that is on Earth. The long-time suffering, misery, and pain of sin will end, and all that are not an enemy of Jesus, those that chose to live in his Kingdom, will be gathered in one and rest in him.

*"For the earnest expectation of the **creature waiteth** for the manifestation of the sons of God. For the creature was made subject to vanity, not willingly, but by reason of him who hath subjected the same in hope, Because the **creature itself also shall be delivered from the bondage of corruption into the glorious liberty of the children of God.** For we know that the **whole creation groaneth and travaileth in pain** together until now."*
Romans 8:19-22

*"That in the dispensation of the fulness of times he might **gather together in one all things in Christ,***

*both which are **in heaven**, and which are **on earth**;*
even in him: In whom also we have obtained an
inheritance, being predestinated according to the
purpose of him who worketh all things after the
counsel of his own will: That we should be to the
praise of his glory, who first trusted in Christ. In
*whom **ye also trusted**, after that ye **heard the word***
***of truth**, the **gospel of your salvation**: in whom*
*also after **that ye believed**, ye were sealed with that*
holy Spirit of promise, Which is the earnest of our
inheritance until the redemption of the purchased
possession, unto the praise of his glory."
Ephesians 1:10-14

Jesus' death on the cross answered every issue that came about from Lucifer's sin and deception to Adam's sin and rebellion, covering both the natural and the spirit realms. Genesis 3:15 is the ultimate prophecy, for it is within these two persons (seeds) that all prophecy of the Bible converges, ending the ancient war for the Kingdom. That is the seed of Satan and the seed of the woman, which ultimately would give birth to Messiah, Jesus.

*"And I will put **enmity between thee and the***
***woman**, and between **thy seed** and **her seed**; it shall*
bruise thy head, and thou shalt bruise his heel."
Genesis 3:15

*"And there was **war in heaven: Michael and his** angels fought against the dragon; and the **dragon fought and his angels.**"*
Revelation 12:7

*"And **the dragon** was wroth with **the woman,** and went to make war with the remnant of her seed, which keep the commandments of God, and have the testimony of Jesus Christ."*
Revelation 12:17

*"I beheld till the thrones were cast down, and the **Ancient of days** did sit, whose garment was white as snow, and the hair of his head like the pure wool: **his throne** was like the **fiery flame,** and his **wheels as burning fire.** A **fiery stream** issued and came forth from before him: thousand thousands ministered unto him, and ten thousand times ten thousand stood before him: the judgment was set, and the books were opened. I beheld then because of the voice of the great words which the horn spake: I beheld even till the **beast was slain,** and his body destroyed, and given to the burning flame. As concerning the **rest of the beasts,** they had their dominion taken away: yet their lives were prolonged for a season and time. I saw in the night visions, and, behold, one **like the Son of man** came with the clouds of heaven, and*

*came to the **Ancient of days,** and they brought him near before him. And there was **given him dominion,** and glory, and a **kingdom,** that all people, nations, and languages, should serve him: **his dominion is an everlasting dominion,** which shall not pass away, and **his kingdom that which shall not be destroyed.***"
Daniel 7:9-14

The beast that was slain is the Antichrist, given to the burning flame or Lake of Fire, the "rest of the beasts," Satan and other fallen angels, will not be destroyed until the end of the Millennial reign. *"And cast him into the **bottomless pit,** and **shut him up,** and set a seal upon him, that he should deceive the nations no more, **till the thousand years should be fulfilled:** and after that he must be loosed a little season." Revelation 20:3*

Psalms 148 gives us an outline of all creation. All are commanded to praise the Lord.

*"Praise ye the LORD. **Praise ye the LORD from the heavens:** praise him in the heights. Praise ye him, all his **angels:** praise ye him, all his **hosts.** Praise ye him, **sun** and **moon:** praise him, all ye **stars** of light. Praise him, ye **heavens** of heavens, and ye **waters that be above the heavens.** Let them praise the name of the LORD: for he*

commanded, and they were created. He hath also stablished them for ever and ever: he hath made a decree which shall not pass.

Praise the LORD from the earth, *ye **dragons**, and all **deeps**: Fire, and hail; snow, and vapour; stormy wind fulfilling his word: Mountains, and all hills; fruitful trees, and all cedars: **Beasts**, and all **cattle; creeping things,** and **flying fowl: Kings of the earth**, and all **people; princes**, and all **judges** of the earth: Both young men, and maidens; old men, and children: Let them praise the name of the LORD: for his name alone is excellent; his glory is above the earth and heaven. He also exalteth the horn of **his people**, the praise of all **his saints;** even of the **children of Israel**, a people near unto him. Praise ye the LORD."*
Psalm 148

EPILOGUE

Rahab's reign as the "god of this world" is rapidly ending, to commence what is known as the Great Tribulation, seven years of judgment and the wrath of God against his enemies. A period so intense that men's hearts will fail them from fear, the sun and stars again withholding their light.

> *"In whom the **god of this world** hath **blinded the minds** of them **which believe not**, lest the light of the glorious gospel of Christ, who is the image of God, should shine unto them."*
> 2 Corinthians 4:4

> *"Men's **hearts failing them for fear**, and for looking after those things which are coming on the earth: for **the powers of heaven shall be shaken.**"*
> Luke 21:26

> *"**The sun and the moon shall be darkened,** and the stars shall **withdraw their shining.** The LORD also shall roar out of Zion, and utter his voice from Jerusalem; and the **heavens and the earth***

shall shake: but the LORD will be the hope of his people, and the strength of the children of Israel."
Joel 3:15-16

Israel's establishment as a nation in 1948 began the prophetic time clock ticking towards the end. In the last couple of years, prophecy and activities of Israel have increased rapidly and will seemingly snowball into the Tribulation. The seven-year Tribulation will see more death and destruction than any time since the creation of Adam. As this book goes to press, Israel is currently at war with Hamas and Hezbollah, promising to become a global conflict in scope and ultimately fulfill many major prophecies. This conflict is the essence and trigger point for the final world war of Gog and Magog (Ezekiel 38) just before the beginning of the Tribulation. Four times in Revelation Jesus says, "I come quickly" possibly meaning that events and prophecies will be fulfilled faster and faster the closer we get to the end. That is precisely what we see today.

*"Behold, **I come quickly**: hold that fast which thou hast, that no man take thy crown."*
Revelation 3:11

*"Behold, **I come quickly**: blessed is he that keepeth the sayings of the prophecy of this book."*
Revelation 22:7

*"And, behold, **I come quickly**; and my reward is with me, to give every man according as his work shall be."*
Revelation 22:12

*"He which testifieth these things saith, Surely **I come quickly**. Amen. Even so, come, Lord Jesus."*
Revelation 22:20

Dear reader, if you want to escape the horrors of the Tribulation and have not put your trust completely in the Lord, then believe in Jesus and choose life, as God has set before every man since the time of Adam, a choice to choose between good and evil, to live for eternity within the Kingdom, within the family of God, or be eternally separated.

*"I call **heaven** and **earth** to record this day against you, that I have set before you **life and death**, **blessing and cursing**: therefore **choose life**, that both thou and thy seed **may live:"***
Deuteronomy 30:19

*"These things have I written unto you that **believe on the name of the Son of God**; that ye may know that ye have **eternal life**, and that ye may believe on the name of the Son of God."*
1 John 5:13

*"All thy works shall praise thee, O LORD; and thy saints shall bless thee. They shall speak of the **glory of thy kingdom**, and talk of thy power; To make known to the sons of men his mighty acts, and **the glorious majesty of his kingdom.** Thy kingdom is an **everlasting kingdom,** and **thy dominion endureth** throughout all generations.*
Psalms 145:10-13

*"And **every creature** which is in **heaven**, and on the **earth**, and under the earth, and such as are in the **sea**, and all that are in them, heard I saying, Blessing, and honour, and glory, and power, be unto him **that sitteth upon the throne**, and unto the **Lamb** for ever and ever."*
Revelation 5:13

SCRIPTURE INDEX

www.ingramcontent.com/pod-product-compliance
Lightning Source LLC
Chambersburg PA
CBHW060935120626
46557CB00003B/1002